Authentic Life Coaching for Youth

7 Steps for Coaching Youth Towards Successful Transition

Ebony Lyons Harris, MAOM

Felisha,
I thank you
for your support
God Bless! :)
Ebony

Copyright © 2015 Ebony Lyons Harris

ALL RIGHTS RESERVED

Without limiting the rights under copyright reserved above, no part of this publication may be reproduced, stored in or introduced into a retrieval system, or transmitted, in any form, or by any means (electronic, mechanical, photocopying, recording, or otherwise), without the prior contractual or written permission of the copyright owner of this work.

.   .   .   .   .

First Edition: December 2015

Printed in the United States of America

ISBN: 978-0-9819611-8-7

Dedication

This book is dedicated to my husband Leonard Jr. and two sons Quin and Jalen who have allowed me to take care of other children as if they were my own. Thank you for allowing me to share my heart with thousands of young people who did not chose a life in foster care.

Special Dedication

To my parents, Gregory & Jeanette Lyons who always support me in everything I do. I am thankful and blessed to have you as parents.

Extra Special Dedication

To Leonard Harris Sr. my father-in-law who always asked "Ebby, when are you going to write that book?" Here it is Dad! May you continue to Rest in Paradise. Thank you for your eternal encouragement and support.

A Reason, a Season, or a Lifetime

People come into your life for a reason, a season, or a lifetime. When you figure out which one it is, you will know what to do. When someone is in your life for a **REASON**, it is usually to meet a need you have expressed. They have come to assist you through a difficulty, to provide you with guidance and support, to aid you physically, emotionally, or spiritually. They may seem like a Godsend, and they are! They are there for the reason you need them to be.

Then, without any wrong doing on your part, or at an inconvenient time, this person will say or do something to bring the relationship to an end. Sometimes they die. Sometimes they walk away. Sometimes they act up and force you to take a stand.

What we must realize is that our need has been met, our desire fulfilled, their work is done. The prayer you sent up has been answered. And now it is time to move on.

When people come into your life for a **SEASON**, it is because your turn has come to share, grow, or learn. They bring you an experience of peace, or make you laugh. They may teach you something you have never done. They usually give you an unbelievable amount of joy. Believe it! It is real! But, only for a season.

LIFETIME relationships teach you lifetime lessons; things you must build upon in order to have a solid emotional foundation. Your job is to accept the lesson, love the person, and put what you have learned to use in all other relationships and areas of your life. It is said that love is blind, but friendship is clairvoyant.

[Author unknown]

Table of Contents

Introduction

Working in the child welfare system for over 20 years I've seen many youth age out of the system with little support and very few skills to live on their own. Youth aging out of foster care often lack the consistent support to help them successfully transition into adulthood thus, leaving them without the ability to navigate through life and have a clear plan for success. This is mainly due to a 'hodge-podge' approach and rush to transition youth out of the 'system'.

What I've learned throughout my career is that young people need and often want guidance, that allows them to make decisions on their own. However, because in most cases they have lacked guidance, things that are viewed as simple and easy are not for transitioning foster youth. They have also experienced the "wrong and gone" effect which is if you do something wrong you are gone. This approach leaves them little room to make and learn from their mistakes. Many years ago, I had a desire to help young people and although I respect my profession, I felt that authentic engagement of youth was missing in the transition process for youth aging out of the system where case   workers are inundated with completing home visits, case plans, placement disruptions, and attending court hearings, there is   little room to support the transitional needs of youth on their caseloads. Thus, Authentic Life Coaching for Youth was birthed.

This approach is designed for people who work in the foster care and youth service professions who would like to acquire new skills and tools to empower youth to take action for their lives. It is unique in that it focuses on the needs for youth transitioning out of the foster care system into adulthood but can be easily used with various transitioning youth and young adult populations. The foundation for this process is based on basic foundational life coaching tenets with a focus on helping youth transition into adult life. The authentic youth coaching process provides a useful framework to guide youth discussion in ways that open up communication and build trust. It also creates a powerful commitment to mutual learning and a partnership for discovering the best next steps.

CHAPTER 1 : Defining Coaching

What is Coaching?

"Coaching is an on-going partnership that helps clients produce fulfilling results in their personal and professional lives. Through the process of coaching, clients deepen their learning, improve their performance, and enhance their quality of life. Beginning with the clients' desires, coaching uses reporting, exploring, and a consistent commitment to move the client forward. Coaching accelerates the clients' progress by providing greater focus and awareness of choice. Coaching concentrates on where clients are today and what they are willing to do to get where they want to be tomorrow."

—International Coach Federation, ICF

Coaching is:

- A partnership that is focused on a client's success.
- An effective means of facilitating transitions, exploring creative solutions and developing clarity to manifest what the client wants in their lives.

Why Life Coaching for Foster Youth?

Most foster youth have received some type of counseling and/or therapy during their life in foster care and are in need of the tools and resources that life coaching provides to move forward. This life coaching model provides a true partnership for the youth that puts them in the driver's seat of their decisions.

What is Authentic Life Coaching for Youth?

Authentic Life Coaching for Youth is a coaching approach for transition aged youth (14-24) that focuses on the unique needs of youth in the foster care system but is relevant to any youth transitioning into adult interdependence. Authentic Life Coaching for Youth is geared toward helping youth service professionals apply a system and develop additional skills to work with youth who are transitioning into adulthood. The Authentic Life Coaching for Youth model is a two-tiered seven-step process that is backed by best practice and evidence informed techniques to provide a unique approach to coaching transition age youth. The first tier focuses the long-range goal and the second tier focuses on the development of the necessary life skills to help the youth achieve the goal.

The seven steps of the Authentic Life Coaching for Youth Model are:

Step 1 – Starting from Bottom
Step 2 – The Vision
Step 3 – Keeping it Real
Step 4 – Got Skills?
Step 5 – Who's Got Your Back?
Step 6 – The Master Plan
Step 7 – Coaching to Achieve G.O.A.L.S.

Authentic Life Coaching for Youth also focuses on the transitions that youth go through as they undergo their own life-shifts. The process seeks to provide youth with support, sharing, encouragement, and goal development/achievement. Authentic Life Coaching for Youth deals mainly with the areas that youth need to focus on to move forward successfully and concentrates on the motivational and life skills development aspects of transition.

What Life Coaching Isn't

A common misconception is that coaching is the same as therapy, when in fact they are quite different. Therapy is intended to help people recover from emotional or other psychological disorders such as depression or anxiety. Therapy or treatment is the attempted mediation of a health/ psychological problem, usually following a diagnosis.

Life coaching isn't counseling or therapy, life coaches are not qualified to diagnose or treat mental health matters. Coaching is intended to help individuals achieve personal goals.

The life coach's primary role is to provide a system that makes it easier for the client to achieve their goals, personally, academically, professionally and socially. Life coaches help their clients identify positive choices, which move their lives forward, and negative choices, which hold them, back.

Therapy	Coaching
Therapy is about healing	Coaching is about achievement
Therapy is about safety	Coaching is about momentum
Therapy is about understanding	Coaching is about action
Therapy is about progress	Coaching is about performance
Therapy is about protecting	Coaching is about attracting
Therapy is about resolving	Coaching is about creating

Life coaching is a practice with the aim of helping clients determine and achieve personal goals. Life coaches use multiple methods that will help clients with the process of setting and reaching goals. Coaching is not targeted at psychological illness and coaches are neither therapists nor consultants. Life coaching has its roots in executive coaching, which drew on techniques developed in management consulting and leadership training. Life coaching also draws inspiration from disciplines including sociology, psychology, positive youth development, career counseling, mentoring and other types of counseling. The life coach may apply mentoring, values assessment, behavior modification, behavior modeling, goal-setting and other techniques in helping their clients.

How Is a Coach Different From a...

Consultant: A consultant usually is a specialist in a given area. They are hired to give advice and provide solutions. A consultant usually works with a client to solve a particular problem. Once the problem is solved, the consultant's job is complete. The consultant usually doesn't get involved with areas outside of their specialty. Coaching uses a more holistic approach. In partnership with the client, the coach examines the situation, co-creates a plan of action, and works side by side to achieve the identified goal(s). The coach does not have to be an expert in the client's life; the client is the expert. The coach collaborates with the client to create a solution using the client's knowledge and answers. The coach does not have the answers; they have the questions that lead to the client finding their own answers.

Therapist: A therapist typically works with a dysfunctional person to get them to functional. A coach works with a functional person to get them to exceptional. Therapists typically work with people who need help becoming emotionally healthy. They often deal with past issues and how to overcome them. A coach works with functional people to move them to exceptional levels. Coaching does not rely on past issues for achieving growth, but on goals for the future. Coaching is action oriented. The focus is on where the client is, where they want to be, and how to get them there. The way to know if you are doing therapy is if you are working in the past, the client is stuck and can't seem to move forward, or there is a drug or alcohol problem, more than likely you are doing something other than coaching. Part of being a good coach is knowing when and when not to coach. If the client needs therapy refer them to a therapist. Clients can use the services of a therapist and a coach at the same time.

Counselor: While a counselor provides information and expertise, the relationship is normally hierarchical, perhaps even authoritarian. The coaching relationship is not hierarchical, the client and the coach partner to create a better future for the client.

Mentor: Mentoring is a relationship that is established with someone that is an expert in their field. The mentor is usually older and more experienced than the mentee. The mentor bestows their knowledge and wisdom onto the mentee. The mentee looks up to the mentor and seeks guidance and advice from the mentor. A coaching relationship is a partnership where the coach walks side by side with the client. The coach supports the client in drawing on their own wisdom and following their inner guidance.

Trainer: Training is about equipping people with new skills and knowledge to help their personal and/or professional development. The skilled trainer will train/teach people the relevant new information and, ideally address all four KASH (Knowledge, Attitudes, Skills and Habits) aspects of their subject area. Although there is a small aspect of equipping in coaching the focus is on assisting the client to identify, improve, and implement new skills and knowledge to improve their life that will assist them with their desired outcomes.

Life Coaching From a Learning to Ride a Bicycle Example

The example of a learning to ride a bicycle and how different professions would support a client in this endeavor is a common example that is used in the coaching community to explain the difference between consulting, counseling, therapy, counseling, training and mentoring.

A therapist would help you discover what is holding you back from riding the bike. They would go back into your past and find out what kind of experience you had at the age of five with a bicycle.

A consultant would bring you a bicycle manual and tell you everything you ever wanted to know about the workings of a bicycle. The consultant would then depart and return in six months to see how you were doing.

A mentor would share their experiences of bike riding and the lessons that they learned. The mentor would bestow all the wisdom they had about bicycle riding upon you.

A trainer would demonstrate how riding a bicycle is done, give you step-by-step instructions, give you the equipment you need, and observe while you were riding giving feedback when needed.

A coach would help you get up on the bicycle, encourage, endorse, acknowledge and support you while running alongside you, until you feel comfortable enough to go it alone.

<u>Notes</u>

CHAPTER 2 : Understanding Transitioning Youth

Aging Out

For tens of thousands of young people in foster care, turning 18 means losing the supports (financial, educational, and social) that they count on. Their peers in the general population receive support from their families throughout emerging adulthood, becoming more independent as their brains develop through age 25. But when young people leave foster care without having a permanent family—when they 'age out'—what should be a gradual transition often becomes an abrupt loss that puts them at risk of negative outcomes.

Since 1999, more than 230,000 young people have transitioned from foster care without permanent family connections. Youth transition without the typical growing-up experiences that teach self-sufficiency skills, and without the family supports and community networks that help them make successful transitions to adulthood. These young people experience very poor outcomes at a much higher rate than the general population.

Below are just a few:

- More than one in five will become homeless after age 18.
- 58 percent will graduate from high school by age 19 (compared to 87 percent of 19 year olds in the general population).
- 71 percent of young women are pregnant by 21, facing higher rates of unemployment, criminal conviction, public assistance, and involvement in the child welfare system.
- At the age of 24, only half have stable employment.
- One in four will be involved in the justice system within two years of leaving the foster care system.

Transitioning from Foster Care

Most young people at age 18 still rely on family and community support to help them transition into adulthood. Foster youth, however, have no permanent family or support network to assist them as they age out of the system, and only limited assistance to support their transition to independence. Many of these young people have limited education, few basic skills and no role models or adult mentors.

Young people leaving foster care face many more challenges than their peers who come from supportive families. Research indicates that four years after leaving foster care, 46 percent of these youth have not finished high school, 25 percent have been homeless, 42 percent have become parents themselves and fewer than 20 percent are completely self-supporting. Census data shows that only 3 percent of young people who age out of the foster care system are likely to finish college, compared with 28 percent of the U.S. general peer population. Young people leaving foster care disproportionately suffer from mental and other health problems.

Young people coming out of the foster care system encounter a number of barriers that limit their opportunities for economic success. First, they often have low educational attainment and little to no work experience, so job opportunities are limited. Second, many of these youth do not have a driver's license, which again limits their job options. Third, many youth do not have access to basic health care. Fourth, they do not have the financial resources needed to secure housing. These young people do not have supportive adults who can co-sign on an apartment lease or help them with rent deposits, so stable housing is always a significant barrier. Finally, these youth have no financial safety net, and many lack basic life and financial management skills. Overcoming these barriers and helping these young people achieve economic success is critical for stabilizing this very vulnerable population.[1]

The Adolescent Brain

Many disciplines have contributed to the knowledge base regarding what enables young people in foster care to succeed. Neuroscience has added critical data to that base by revealing that in adolescence, the brain experiences a period of major development comparable to that of early childhood.

Among the implications of the new data is this: Adolescents must take on distinct developmental tasks in order to move through emerging adulthood and become healthy, connected, and productive adults and young people in foster care often lack the supports needed to complete these tasks. Unlike younger children in foster care, for whom safety and protection are the greatest need, older youth are in the process of developing greater autonomy and practicing adult roles and responsibilities. It is during adolescence and early adulthood that we develop a personal sense of identity, establish emotional and psychological independence, establish adult vocational goals, learn to manage

---

[1]Transitioning Youth From Foster Care to Successful Adulthood. Partners (Number 2, 2007) www.frbatlanta.org/

sexuality and sexual identity, adopt a personal value system, and develop increased impulse control and behavioral maturity. Chemical changes in the brain that prime adolescents for risk-taking present rich opportunities for them to learn from experience and mistakes and, with adult support, gain greater self-regulation, coping, and resiliency skills.

The emerging science of adolescent brain development has deepened the understanding of adolescent capabilities and behaviors. Neuroscience has made it clear that the brain is not "done" by age 6 as was previously believed. Instead, the adolescent brain continues to develop, providing a window of opportunity similar to that, which is open in early childhood. Adolescence is a period of "use it or lose it" in brain development. Young people's experiences during this period play a critical role in shaping their futures as adults. They can build and practice resiliency and develop knowledge and skills that will positively serve them throughout adulthood.

Recent research has helped us understand the adolescent brain in new and powerful ways. Because of this research, it is now widely understood that young people between the ages of 14 and 25 must take on distinct social and developmental tasks to become healthy, connected, and productive adults. Young people, who are removed from these tasks or prevented from taking them on, have greater difficulty achieving success in school, work and life. Young people in foster care too often face these unnecessary barriers to success.

Young people in foster care have often experienced a range of stressful and traumatic experiences. With this new research it was found that there is a window of time, to counteract the damage caused by those experiences. Adolescence is that time and it offers tremendous opportunity for young people. When the adolescent brain is exposed to developmentally healthy experiences, it can actually "rewire" itself. This can help any young person, regardless of prior trauma, get on a better path to a bright future.

Many young people in foster care, especially those who abruptly age out of the foster care system at age 18, lack access to a supportive family or network. Healthy relationships are critical to coping with the stressful and traumatic experiences that foster youth too often face. Transition age youth need supportive, age appropriate transitional supportive services that more closely mirror the experiences of young people in supportive, intact families.[2]

Emotional Stages & Transition

There are two types of stages and changes as it relates to youth transitioning. There are the emotional changes and the transitional shifts. As a young person prepares to move out on his/her own or is living on their own, you can expect them to go through four distinct *emotional* stages. The four stages are anxiety, elation, fear and loneliness, and quiet confidence. It is important that the life coach is able to recognize these stages and help youth work through them.

The Bridges Transition Model focuses on **transition** not change. The difference between these is subtle but important to distinguish. Change is something that happens to people, even if they don't agree with it. Transition, on the other hand, is internal; it's what happens in people's minds as they go through change. Change can happen very quickly, while transition usually occurs more slowly. Combining the four emotional stages with the Bridges Transition Model will help you recognize these transitional changes as you coach.

---

[2]The Adolescent Brain: New Research and Its Implications for Young People Transitioning From Foster Care © 2011, Jim Casey Youth Opportunities Initiative

Four Emotional Stages of Transition

Anxiety: During this stage youth have to "let go" of significant adults and resources. They have numerous fears about moving out on their own. They begin to question their readiness for living on their own. The first stage is that of anxiety. The youth is anxious about two uncertainties. The first is whether or not the adults in his/her life will actually let him/her move out. The second relates to whether she/he has what it takes to make it. The youth is looking for 'permission' to leave or validation and a truthful answer to the question, "I'm ready, aren't I? It is part of the life coach's role to give good, honest feedback, to let youth know when they are ready and when they are not and to encourage them. 'Permission' should not come too easily and should be based on a youth's readiness, both financially and emotionally to take on the challenge. When it is clear that a youth is not ready, then the life coach's role it is to help them identify ways and skills to become ready. Life coaches can help minimize anxiety by showing youth the steps they can take that will lead them to readiness. Such steps include learning how to get and keep a job, learning how to manage money, learning how to problem solve, and learning all of the other skills that are essential to self-sufficiency.

Elation: This phase is short lived usually lasting about a month. Youth tend to "feel free" in their apartment, away from adult control. However, living on your own requires being responsible for all bills, house cleaning, developing a routine, and etc. Youth need strong emotional support during this time from caring adults to help them cope with disappointment. It is exciting to anticipate independence, which is often defined by youth as freedom. Being on your own, in your own place, with your own things is a thrilling experience, at least in the beginning. When a young person is experiencing this stage of elation, it is your job to keep the young person grounded. The daily chores must still be done. The bills must be paid. The balance of work and/ or school must be maintained.

Fear and Loneliness: Again, the elation stage doesn't last long as young people realize that independence is not all that they envisioned. Maintaining a household routine of paying bills, cooking and household management are boring and sometimes difficult. Friends are not as available and it is difficult to make new ones. The paycheck doesn't go as far as she/he thought it would. A roommate moves out leaving him/her stuck with the rent. His/her friends have moved away or have jobs with different work hours. When these unsettling situations occur (and they will) the youth moves into a stage of depression characterized by fear and loneliness. Life becomes upsetting. It's annoying to have to wash the dishes every day and keep the place clean. There's not enough money to go out and have fun as often as before. Old friends seem to disappear and new friends have yet to be made. There are too many things that have to be done and not enough things that they want to do. The danger in this stage is that the youth may start cutting classes, drop out of school or lose his/her job. Young people can withdraw and become isolated.

The life coach's role during this stage is to keep the youth moving forward. Ensuring that youth are taking care of those mundane chores that must be taken care of and keeping a daily routine. A life coach can also serve as an important bridge during this time as the youth moves from old acquaintances to new ones. The life coach may be the only person that remains constant during this time of change.

Quiet confidence: the onset of this stage is subtle and it may take some time to realize that the youth has in fact reached this plateau. When he/she calls you it is after crisis has been averted or already dealt with. The phone call is to tell you what she/he did about the situation. He/She is no longer asking for your advice. Our job during this stage is to either separate/terminate or to develop an adult – adult relationship with which both can be comfortable.Youth "check in" with their support networks to discuss how they have resolved a particular situation. Young people are developing new and lasting relationships and their life experiences are producing accomplishments.

Three Stages of Transition

The Bridges model has three stages of transition that people go through when they experience change. These are:

1. Ending, Losing, and Letting Go.
2. The Neutral Zone.
3. The New Beginning

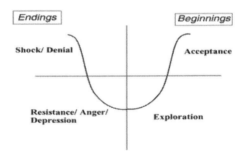

Stage 1: Ending, Losing, and Letting Go

Youth enter this initial stage of transition when you first present them with change. This stage is often marked with resistance and emotional upheaval, because people are being forced to let go of something that they are comfortable with. Youth have to accept that something is ending before they can begin to accept the new idea. If a coach doesn't acknowledge the emotions that the youth is going through, you'll likely encounter resistance throughout the entire coaching process.

At this stage, people may experience these emotions:

Fear	Disorientation
Denial	Frustration
Anger	Uncertainty
Sadness	A Sense of Loss

Stage 2: The Neutral Zone

In this stage, youth affected by the change are often confused, uncertain, and impatient. Depending on how well you're coaching the youth through the change, they may also experience being overloaded as they get used to new ways of doing things. Think of this phase as the bridge between the old and the new; in some ways, youth will still be attached to the old, while they are also trying to adapt to the new. Despite these, this stage can also be one of great creativity, innovation, and renewal. This is a great time to encourage young people to try new ways of thinking or working.

Here, youth might experience:

- Resentment towards the change
- Low morale and low productivity
- Anxiety about their role, status or identity
- Skepticism about the change

Stage 3: The New Beginning

The last transition stage is a time of acceptance and energy. Youth have begun to embrace the change. They're building the skills they need to work successfully in the new way, and they're starting to see early wins from their efforts.

At this stage, people are likely to experience:

- High energy
- Openness to learning
- Renewed commitment to their role and responsibility

Notes

CHAPTER 3:
Best Practices for Working with Transitioning Youth

Positive Youth Development

Positive youth development is especially critical for young people in care who may be experiencing developmental delays as a result of trauma and loss. Adolescence is a period of "use it or lose it" in brain development: When young people are actively engaged in positive relationships and opportunities to contribute, create, and lead, they "use it" to develop their skills to become successful adults. It is through the formation of internal and external assets, including family and community that young people thrive. Multiple positive relationships are essential in supporting them in achieving their unique aspirations.

Positive youth development is the ongoing process in which all youth are engaged in attempting to meet their basic personal and social needs and build skills and competencies that allow them to function and contribute in their daily lives. Positive youth development for transitioning youth is accomplished through services, opportunities, and supports. *Services* are the provision of resources, goods and knowledge to young people. **Opportunities** is the availability for young people to learn how to operate in the world around them, opportunities to test out ideas and behaviors and experiment with different roles. The roles must be perceived as challenging and legitimate to young people. These are tasks that are taken on and done by the young person not things that are done to or for them. **Supports** are the interpersonal relationships that allow a young person to take full advantage of existing services and opportunities. Supports must be affirming and respectful, ongoing, and offered by a variety of people. Supports are done with young people rather than for them. Coaching can offer a variety of supports by helping youth develop support networks, provide strategic mentors to explore interests and provide activities that allow youth to interact with adults.

There are three types of support that youth need to able to achieve their goals. The first type is **emotional**; emotional support provides a young person with caring individuals to help them meet their needs and discuss issues in a safe environment. The second type of support is **motivation**; motivational support provides high expectations, guidance and/or boundaries. The third is **strategic** support; strategic support helps young people access resources necessary to build competencies to do things for themselves in a supportive environment.

A positive youth development approach to life coaching is an on-going process of meeting the needs of young people by:

- Valuing young people, regardless of their situation.
- Recognizing the strengths and potential of each youth.
- Involving youth in the decisions and processes that affect their lives.
- Promoting a young person's development rather than identifying and fixing their problems.
- Enabling young people to participate in and contribute to

programs and communities.
- Emphasizing services and supports that contribute to healthy development.
- Including a wide range of community members and resources to enhance supports and opportunities for youth.

The Qualities of Positive Youth Development

Youth Feel Physically and Emotionally Safe - Young people will learn better and participate more fully when they feel physically and emotionally safe. This environment encourages honesty, trust, and respect among youth and adults.

Youth Experience Belonging and Ownership - Youth feel included and motivated when they have significant roles as participants and leaders.

Youth Develop Self-Worth - Through meaningful contribution, young people feel free to contribute, their contributions are accepted, acknowledged and appreciated.

Youth Discover Self - Youth are encouraged to try new things and learn about themselves. As a result they discover and practice their interests and skills, test their independence, and take control of their lives.

Youth Develop Quality Relationships with Peers and Adults - Youth develop caring and trusting relationships. Youth and adults learn to respect one another.

Recognizing and Addressing Adult'ism' [3]

Adult'ism' happens when adults hold negative views about young people (prejudice) and can exert power and control over their lives. Adult'ism' also occurs when an adult (or group of adults) holds a negative view of young people as well as having control over what the young people are able to do.

It involves prejudice plus social power. Prejudice is a set of negative beliefs about an entire group of people. Social Power occurs when groups of people have access to the resources it needs to get what it wants, and influence over people. It is important to recognize the fact that adult'ism' can manifest itself in our work and relationships with young people. It is perpetuated by youth's reaction to the behavior and attitudes of adults. As a result, we see the emergence of a cycle.

Here are some adult 'ism' challenges that may hinder the life coaching process:

- General stereotypes about young people being lazy, uneducated, not intelligent, angry, self-absorbed, and silly.
- Young people being left out of decisions being made. Often, those decisions directly affect young people's lives.
- Adults often fail to support young people's development by not supporting opportunities for them to learn through experience.
- Adults often do not ask young people to reflect on the important connections between people, community, and themselves.

---

[3]http://www.hunter.cuny.edu/socwork/nrcfcpp/pass/learning-circles/

How Adult'ism' Manifests

There are three ways that adult 'ism' manifests itself in relationships with youth:

1. Dysfunctional Rescuing
2. Blaming the Victim
3. Avoidance of Contact

When adult'ism' manifests itself in **Dysfunctional Rescuing**, adults help youth because they assume that he/she cannot help him/herself.

- Possible responses include always allowing adults to take the lead, youth are set up to fail, and they lose opportunities to take on challenges.
- Young people also learn to "Beat the System". This occurs when a young person who is "rescued" learns to beat the system by manipulating others through guilt, anger, pretending to be ignorant, or being invisible.

The alternative behavior to dysfunctional rescuing is **Functional Helping**. It is important for adults to resist doing things for youth. It is important to let them learn from their experiences. Adults should provide clear and consistent feedback on both positive behavior and areas that need improvement. Youth must be actively involved in planning their future. They should have a voice and choice in the planning process.

Another way that Adult'ism' manifests itself is **Blaming the Victim** approach; this is when adults blame the problems of a young person on the young person without consideration to other factors in the environment. Youth learn to blame the system because they are accustomed to being blamed throughout their lives. Youth will typically not take responsibility for their actions and blame others. As a result, young people do not get the support that they need and lose motivation to participate. Some alternative behaviors to blaming the victim include learning more about the current situation, listening with respect to their concerns without putting them down and including them in goal setting. The alternative strategy for combating Blaming the Victim is **Taking Responsibility** by looking at how our own thoughts and behaviors contribute to situations, giving youth responsibility for determining actions that affect their lives, and becoming more aware of the standards used to assess youth.

Adult'ism' also manifests itself in **Avoidance of Contact**. Adults avoid social or profession contact. It's not surprising that youth learn to Avoid Contact with adults, which occurs when youth respond to avoidance by avoiding back. They tend to distrust adults. Young people become alienated from adults and come to believe that adults have little to offer them. It also diminishes trust for both the adult and youth.

Alternate responses to Avoidance of Contact include spending more time getting to know youth, being open to changing your perceptions to fit your new experiences with youth, and creating shared experiences with youth. The strategy for combating Avoidance of Contact is the alternative behavior of **Making Contact.**

Strategies for Combating Adult'ism'

Adult'ism'	Alternate Response	Strategies
Dysfunctional Rescuing	Functional Helping	• Resist doing things for young people that they can do for themselves • Provide clear and constructive feedback that notes positive behaviors as well as areas for improvement • Engage young people as partners in formulating plans for improvement of their lives or behaviors
Blaming the Victim	Taking Responsibility	• Take responsibility for determining your own standards • Define how your own thoughts & behaviors contribute to a situation • Do not degrade the concerns or issues of any person or group of people • Do not assess a youth by using the standards of your own group
Avoiding Contact	Making Contact	• Make an effort to learn about the lives and concerns of people who are different from yourself • Make an effort to get to know and interact personally with people who are different from yourself • Be willing to change your perceptions to fit your new experiences.

How to Actively Address Adult'ism'

Develop **awareness**, which involves learning about how people are different from and similar to you. When working one to one with youth, it is important to learn about their cultural heritage, beliefs, interests, strengths and needs.

Developing **sensitivity**, which involves developing supportive attitudes, feelings, values, and/or beliefs about other people. Differences between people are not right or wrong, better or worse, more or less intelligent. They are just simply differences.

Competency involves a lifelong process of learning. This process includes developing skills to understand and appreciate differences and similarities within, among, and between groups.

The Spectrum of Youth-Adult Partnership

As an adult in true partnership with young people, you must work differently than most adults did when they worked with you as a youth. You need to examine where your attitudes toward partnership with young people came from, what attitudes underly your actions and think about how that needs to change or stay the same. The attitudes that adults hold toward young people often determine the degree to which they involve them as significant partners in decision making.

In his spectrum of adult attitudes, William Lofquist categorizes work with young people as fitting into one of three categories. Lofquist developed a *Spectrum of Attitudes* that highlights the three different approaches adults take toward working with young people, namely; Youth as Objects, Youth as Recipients, and Youth as Resources.

Youth As Objects: In this approach, which is similar to adult'ism' the attitude is that young people have little to contribute. Adults may truly believe that they need to protect young people from 'suffering' from their mistakes. However, we know that involvement in meaningful roles is essential to positive growth and development of successful young adults. The "youth as objects" approach means that things are being done *to* and *for* youth.

Object Approach Statements:

- *"Let's schedule you for life skills class."*
- *"The case plan says this is what we are going to do next."*
- *"Department policy prohibits youth from determining which family members they can maintain contact with."*
- *"All foster youth must attend group life skills class."*
- *"You are not allowed to set your own curfew due to group home rules."*

Youth As Recipients: In this approach, the attitude is that young people need to be guided through their participation in adult society. Adults "allowing" young people to take part in the decision-making process characterize this attitude. The adults believe the experience will be "good for them" and an excellent opportunity for the youth to practice for when they become "real people." Consequently, responsibilities and tasks often delegated to young people are either trivial (it won't matter if they mess up) or those which adults don't want to do. The result? Youth realize that their role remains trivial and that adults are retaining the position of authority and much of the responsibility.

The "youth as recipients" approach is often confusing. Many adults think they have gotten youth involved or are partners with youth when the youth are really recipients. Services are provided for them and decisions are made for them. Again, they are having things done to and for them, not with and by them.

Recipient Approach Statements:

- *"It will be good for you to attend."*
- *"Counseling will help you see that you cannot live with your mother."*
- *"The court order says you need counseling before making a home visit."*
- *"That was a good lesson for you to learn."*
- *"Our daily house schedule will help you learn responsibility and cooperation."*

Youth As Partners (or Youth as Resources, as originally termed by Lofquist):In this approach, the attitude is that the contributions of young people are welcomed and valued. Adults feel that young people are critical to the success of a program or service. Adults who view young people as partners are comfortable working with groups that have equal members of youth and adults. As full partners, both youth and adults bring strengths to the table and work in an equitable relationship.

Partner Approach Statements:

- "What is your opinion on the situation?"
- "I would like for you to talk with your roommate about decorating your apartment."
- "What do you need to have a successful home visit?"
- "Would you be willing to facilitate our next coaching session?"
- "Please share your ideas on how we can better meet your needs."
- "How do you plan to get your chores done while holding down a full-time job?"

In your coaching it is important to recognize how you as a coach interact with youth from this perspective and how they are accustomed to being dealt with. First from your perspective recognize in your interactions and even prior to work with youth how you have worked with them as objects (you control), recipients (you deliver) or partners (you collaborate). From the youth's perspective based on how they respond to you in coaching, as objects (they ask you to 'just tell them what to do') recipients (they wait on you to 'give them the plan') or partners (they work with you collaboratively to develop 'their next steps'). Once you recognize this you are aware and able to shift into partnership mode.

Authentic Youth - Adult Partnership [4]

Engaging adolescents in planning and decision-making regarding their own lives and the larger community reaps critical benefits throughout the process of transitioning to adulthood. As referenced in the previous section, there is emerging knowledge in the field of neuroscience tells us that during adolescence and young adulthood the brain is undergoing extensive remodeling and that experience plays a critical role in how the brain matures. Again, the concept is one of "use it or lose it" as brain synapses that see little use wither away and those that are used become stronger.

Young people who have opportunities to be fully engaged with adults and "practice" adult skills such as reasoning, decision-making, and self-regulation are thus strengthening the parts of the brain responsible for those functions. Young people in foster care have often been removed from natural opportunities for decision making, community engagement, and leadership and they experience a sense of powerlessness and isolation. The intentional creation of leadership and engagement

---

[4]Transitions: The Rights. Respect. Responsibility.® Campaign Volume 14, No. 1, October 2001

in coaching is therefore particularly important for this group of young people. The engagement of young people succeeds best when it is authentic and when it is supported by youth-adult partnerships.

Why Authenticity is Important

While it is often claimed that young people are being engaged, not all engagement of young people is authentic. Engagement loses authenticity when adults are conflicted about questions of power and control. The attitudes adults hold about young people influence the ability of youth-adult partnerships to be effective and for youth engagement to be authentic. Young people can also hold stereotypes about adults that impact youth-adult partnerships as well. It is therefore critical to address the attitudes and beliefs that each person holds about the other.

What is Authentic Youth Engagement?[5]

Youth engagement has been defined as "young people who are actively and authentically involved, motivated, and excited about the process to move them forward in a positive way.

Authentic youth engagement can best be described by focusing on the experiences of young people when they are engaged:

- They are respected, valued, and trusted and they feel appreciated, safe, and comfortable.
- They feel they are working in an environment that facilitates their engagement, and they are involved in a meaningful way as teachers as well as students.
- Their voices are being heard and treated as worthwhile.
- They are given the opportunity to be involved and make

---

[5]Authentic Youth Engagement: Youth-Adult Partnerships
http://www.jimcaseyyouth.org/authentic-youth-engagement-youth-adult-partnerships

decisions, gain leadership skills, and see their ideas realized.

- They are able to participate in the social aspects of their involvement.
- They see change and progress happening as a result of their contributions.
- They are in a space where they have ownership and control in decision making processes.

CHAPTER 4: Coaching Techniques

Powerful Coaching Questions

The purpose of power coaching questions is to help the youth focus on their issues or ambitions with a totally different perspective. Powerful questions are provocative queries that put a halt to evasion and confusion. By asking powerful questions, the coach invites the client to clarity, action, and discovery at a whole new level. As you can see from the following examples, these generally are open-ended questions that create greater possibility for expanded learning and fresh perspective.

When using open-ended questioning you want to utilize powerful coaching questions to keep the coaching session progressive. Utilizing powerful coaching questions coupled with Motivational Interviewing techniques will help build the foundation for the coaching relationship.

It is important to use powerful questions throughout the coaching relationship to continue to put the youth in the control of their decisions.

Below is a list of powerful coaching questions to use in various coaching situations:

Starting the Session

What's occurred since we last spoke?
What would you like to talk about?
What's new/the latest/the update?
How was your week? Where are you right now?

Clarification

What do you mean?
What does it feel like?
What is the part that is not yet clear?
Can you say more? What do you want?

Elaboration

Can you tell me more? What else?
What other ideas/thoughts/feelings do you have about it?

Anticipation

What is possible?
What if it works out exactly as you want it to?
What is the dream?
What is exciting to you about this?

Evaluation

What is the opportunity here?
What is the challenge?
How does this fit with your plans/goals?
What do you think that means?
What is your assessment?

For Instance

If you could do it over again, what would you do differently?

If it had been you, what would you have done?

How else could a person handle this?

If you could do anything you wanted, what would you do?

Fun as Perspective

What does fun mean to you?

What was humorous about the situation?

How can you make this more fun?

How do you want it to be?

If you were to teach people how to have fun, what would you say?

History

What caused it?

What led up to it?

What have you tried so far?

What will you have to do to get the job done?

What support do you need to accomplish it?

What will you do? When will you do it?

Integration

What will you take away from this?

How do you explain this to yourself?

What was the lesson?

How can you make sure you remember what you have learned?

How would you pull all this together?

Learning

If your life depended on taking action, what would you do?

If you had free choice in the matter, what would you do?

If the same thing came up again, what would you do?

If we could wipe the slate clean, what would you do?

If you had it to do over again, what would you do?

Options

What are the possibilities?

If you had your choice, what would you do?

What are possible solutions?

What will happen if you do, and what will happen if you don't?

What options can you create?

Outcomes

What do you want?

What is your desired outcome?

If you got it, what would you have?

How will you know you have reached it?

What would it look like?

Perspective

When you are ninety-five years old, what will you want to say about your life?

What will you think about this five years from now?

How does this relate to your life purpose?

In the bigger scheme of things, how important is this?

Planning

What do you plan to do about it? What is your game plan?

What kind of plan do you need to create?

How do you suppose you could improve the situation?

Now what?

Predictions

How do you suppose it will all work out?
What will that get you? Where will this lead? What are the chances of success?
What is your prediction?

Resources

What resources do you need to help you decide?
What do you know about it now?
How do you suppose you can find out more about it?
What resources are available to you?

Substance

What seems to be the trouble?
What seems to be the main obstacle?
What is stopping you?
What concerns you the most about?
What do you want?

Summary

What is your conclusion?
How is this working?
How would you describe this?
What do you think this all amounts to?
How would you summarize the effort so far?

Taking Action

What action will you take? And after that?
What will you do? When?
Is this a time for action? What action?
Where do you go from here? When will you do that?
What are your next steps?
By what date or time will you complete these steps?

Motivational Interviewing

Motivational Interviewing (MI) is an evidence-based approach that addresses ambivalence to change. Motivational interviewing is non-judgmental, non-confrontational and non-adversarial. Ambivalence is a natural state of uncertainty that each of us experiences throughout most change processes (e.g., dieting; exercising; maintaining health). Ambivalence occurs because of conflicting feelings about the process and outcomes of change. Even though ambivalence is natural, many of us are not aware of it. In addition, many service provider professions have not been trained to respond to people who are ambivalent about change, and most service programs are not designed to accept and work with people who are ambivalent.

The approach attempts to increase the youth's awareness of the potential problems caused, consequences experienced, and risks faced as a result of the behavior in question. Alternately, coaches help youth envision a better future, and become increasingly motivated to achieve it. Either way, the strategy seeks to help youth think differently about their behavior and ultimately to consider what might be gained through change. Motivational interviewing focuses on the present, and entails working with a client to access motivation to change a particular behavior, that is not consistent with a client's personal value or goal. The main goals of motivational interviewing are to engage clients, elicit change talk, and evoke motivation to make positive changes.

Change may occur quickly or may take considerable time, and the pace of change will vary from client to client. Knowledge alone is usually not sufficient to motivate change within a client, and challenges in maintaining change should be thought of as the rule, not the exception. Ultimately, coaches must recognize that motivational interviewing involves collaboration not confrontation, evocation not education, autonomy rather than authority, and exploration instead of explanation. Effective processes for positive change focus on goals that are small, important to the youth, specific, realistic, and oriented in the present and/or future.

The basic approach to interactions in motivational interviewing is captured by the acronym OARS: (1) Open-ended questions, (2) Affirmations, (3) Reflective listening and (4) Summaries. The acronym provides a nice image. It gives us power to move, yet it is not a powerboat.

Open-Ended questions are simply questions that cannot be answered with a "yes", "no" or "three times in the last week". An open-ended powerful questions allow the youth to create the impetus for forward movement. Although close-ended questions have their place and are quite valuable at times, the open-ended question creates a forward momentum that we wish to use in helping the client explore change.

Open-ended questions:

- Who is the most important person in your life? Why is she/he important to you?
- What are the 5 most important things in your life?
- How can I help you with___?
- What was the best 5 minutes of your day? What was the worst 5 minutes of your day?
- How would you like things to be different?
- What are the good things about___ and what are the not so good things about it?
- What do you think you will lose if you give up___?
- What have you tried before to make a change?
- Who are those in your life who will support your changing this behavior?
- What do you want to do next?

Affirmations can be wonderful rapport builders. For youth who have been through serious trauma, affirmations can be a rare commodity. However, they must be congruent and authentic.

Affirming responses:

- I appreciate that you were willing to share that with me.
- You are clearly a very resourceful person.
- You handled yourself really well in that situation.
- That's a good suggestion!
- Congratulations on the successful completion of...
- I really enjoyed this discussion today.
- You are very courageous to be so open about this.
- You've accomplished a lot in a short time.

Reflective listening is the key to this process. The best motivational advice you can give is to listen carefully to your clients. They will tell you what has worked and what hasn't. What moved them forward and shifted them backward. Whenever you are in doubt about what to do, listen. But remember this is a directive approach.

Reflective listening is a communication strategy involving two key steps: seeking to understand a speaker's idea, then offering the idea back to the youth, to confirm the idea has been understood correctly. It attempts to "reconstruct what the youth is thinking and feeling and to relay this understanding back to the youth". Reflective listening is a more specific strategy than the more general methods of active listening. It is the pathway for engaging the client in relationship, building trust, and fostering motivation to change. Reflective listening appears deceptively easy, but it takes hard work and skill to do well. It is vital to learn to think reflectively. This is a way of thinking that accompanies good reflective listening that includes interest in what the person has to say and respect for the person's inner wisdom. What you think the person means may not be what they really mean.

Reflective listening is meant to close the loop in communication to ensure breakdowns don't occur. The listener's voice turns down at the end of a reflective listening statement. This may feel presumptuous, yet it leads to clarification and greater exploration, whereas questions tend to interrupt the client's flow.

Reflective Listening statements:

- So you feel...
- It sounds like you...
- You're wondering if...
- So, what I hear you saying is...
- Thus what I am hearing: please correct me if I am wrong...

Summaries are a feedback loop in the coaching session that keep the understanding clear. This is really just a specialized form of reflective listening where you reflect back to the youth what he/she has been telling you. Summaries are an effective way to communicate your interest in a client, build rapport, and call attention to important elements of the discussion and to shift attention or direction. If the interaction is going in an unproductive or problematic direction (e.g., reinforcing status quo talk, encountering resistance), the summary can be used to shift the focus of the conversation.

Summary Statements; (Begin with a statement indicating you are making a summary):

- Let me see if I understand this so far...
- Here is what I've heard. Tell me if I've missed anything.
- What you've said is important.
- I value what you say.
- Did I hear you correctly?

- We covered that well. Now let's talk about...

The goal in MI is to create forward momentum and to then harness that momentum to create change. Reflective listening keeps that momentum moving forward.

Questions tend to cause a shift in momentum and can stop it entirely. Although there are times you will want to create a shift or stop momentum, most times you will want to keep it flowing.

While there are as many variations in technique, the spirit of the method, however, is more enduring and can be characterized in a few key points:

- Motivation to change is elicited from the client, and is not imposed from outside forces.
- It is the client's task, not the coach's, to articulate and resolve his/her ambivalence.
- Direct persuasion is not an effective method for resolving ambivalence.
- The coaching style is generally quiet and elicits information from the client.
- The coach is directive, in that they help the client to examine and resolve ambivalence.
- Readiness to change is not a trait of the client, but a fluctuating result of interpersonal interaction.
- The coaching relationship resembles a partnership.

Giving Feedback

Feedback is a way to help youth consider changing their behavior. It communicates how effective their actions appear to be and helps them keep their behavior "on target," thus better achieving their goals. There are two criteria for useful feedback. Feedback must be:

Essential

- Feedback is descriptive rather than judgmental.
- Feedback is specific rather than general. To make a general statement about people's behavior, as a whole doesn't tell them which parts of their behavior need changing or which are strengths.
- Feedback is directed at behavior the receiver can do something about.
- Being reminded of shortcomings people can't control will only cause frustration.

Helpful

- Feedback is checked to ensure clear communication. What the giver intends to say is not necessarily equal to its impact on the receiver. It's important to ask about the meaning of anything that's unclear.
- Feedback is both positive and negative. A balanced description of behavior takes both the strong and weak points into account. Both give the other person information for change.
- Feedback takes into account the needs of both the receiver and the giver of the feedback. What you say to people reflects not only what they do, but also its effect on you.
- Feedback is most useful when given immediately after the behavior has occurred.

CHAPTER 5 : 7 Steps for Coaching Youth Towards Successful Transition

Step 1 - Starting From the Bottom

This is where you set the coaching foundation. According to a coaching frame of reference, all clients are to be considered an intelligent and well-informed people. Coaches believe that clients knows all there is to know on the technical dimensions of their issues, either to solve their own problem or to achieve higher performing results than they have in the past. This is also true for youth. Although youth may lack some life experience and foster youth sometimes may not have been provided opportunities to demonstrate age appropriate skills, they are very coachable when they are authentically engaged. The coaching process rests on this frame of reference, and all coach behavior and interactions, including coaching questions, should reflect that frame of reference.

During a coaching process and without any exception, each and every client can and must be considered to be an "expert" in his/her life. In coaching relationships, each client is perceived as answers to achieve his/her personal or professional goals.

This is the most important step in the Authentic Life Coaching model because this step creates the groundwork for all of the following steps. Setting the foundation includes the following components:

- Creating a Safe Coaching Space
- Building Rapport
- Develop an Authentic Youth – Adulthood Partnership
- Designing an Alliance
- Solidifying the Coaching Relationship with a Formal Agreement

Creating a Safe Coaching Space

Creating a safe space is an essential component of coaching relationship that aims to enhance positive youth development. Coaches should aim to create a space that is supportive and provides an experiential learning environment for youth. A comfortable setting should be provided to meet with the young person. This setting also should provide privacy and confidentiality for trust and protection of the young person. This could be accomplished in many settings, but consideration must be used to make sure these elements are incorporated.

To ensure that a safe space is promoted a variety of factors and coaching activities need to be given attention to when providing coaching services to young people. Features that have been identified to likely promote a safe space in coaching include physical and psychological safety, clear and consistent structure, opportunities to contribute, ethical practice, anonymity and a level behavior management.

Building Rapport

Rapport is defined as a close and harmonious relationship in which the people or groups concerned understand each other's feelings or ideas and communicate well. Rapport is special in a coaching relationship. Rapport is one of the active ingredients of coaching that makes it work. Rapport between the coach and youth will typically make the coaching go more smoothly later down the line. Less rapport will make it less effective. What this means is that more time spent by the coach and the youth up front to establish rapport will lead to less effort later to produce results. Less effort up front to create rapport will mean more effort is needed later to stimulate the youth to action.

Here are ways rapport can be built by the coach:

Be curious: Ask a lot of questions. Youth trust people who are interested in them. The reason for this is that youth tend to feel isolated, as life gets more complicated. And when someone pays attention to them they feel safer and less isolated. As a coach the more you use curious information gathering to build rapport the more likely youth will trust you and be coachable.

Be an open space listener: When you ask a question deliberately pause to let the youth answer. This is a sign of respect, which builds feelings of safety and trust. It is the same in building rapport. To build trust you must patiently provide an empty space for the answer to fill. Patient open space listening produces respect, an absence of vulnerability and increases rapport.

Be a flexible mirror: To make someone you're talking to feel comfortable it is helpful to mirror their demeanor. If they are slow and deliberate they will feel most comfortable if you are the same way. If you're in a hurry they will feel uncomfortable and less safe. When trying to mirror someone look for his/her language pattern. Is it deliberate or fast? Try to measure their breathing pattern in the same way. Is it fast or slow? Reflect it. Watch out for their body language. If they are relaxed, don't lean in aggressively. Being flexible in how you act around your coaching clients will help you to be a better coach. It will help you build rapport, their feelings of safety and their receptiveness to your coaching.

Be Focused: Focusing intently on them will build rapport. It will make them feel important and make it easier for them to trust you and this trust will make them more receptive to your coaching. In order to focus intently on them get into a quiet space to coach. This should be away from distractions. Make it easy on yourself to focus. For example, don't coach somewhere where there is a lot of action going in the background. If necessary, face a wall with your client in front of you to make it easy on yourself. If you are distracted during the coaching session it is like saying your client is of less importance than what is distracting.

Be Understanding: Another way to build rapport is let the youth know that you understand where they are coming from. When you acknowledge them, you say and demonstrate that you understand, it doesn't mean you agree it just means that you have heard them. This creates an absence of vulnerability because young people want to know that they have been heard. That makes them feel important and makes it easier to trust.

Show Respect: Never ridicule or humiliate a youth. Recognize each youth is different, and adjust expectations accordingly. Don't play favorites or otherwise allow a youth to perceive that you don't like him and be very careful with sarcasm.

Be Patient: With some youth, building strong rapport can seem to take forever. That's okay. Youth need the freedom to develop relationships at a pace that's comfortable for them. Take your cues from their timeline.

Be Authentic: Don't pretend to be something you're not. Youth respect adults who are authentic, and see right through those who try to act like kids themselves in a misguided effort to be perceived as "cool." We want youth to be proud of who they are and stay true to themselves: why should they expect any different from their life coach?

Stick to Your Word: If you say you'll do it, do it. No questions asked. Youth often need to see your integrity in action before they can develop trust. By doing this you are setting a wonderful example of strong character.

Be Consistent: Knowing what to expect helps reduce anxiety and gives youth a sense of control over their environment.

Show a Little Faith: Youth need strong advocates. Often, they doubt themselves and what they can do. Having an ally in the form of a caring, supportive life coach can help youth achieve things they never dreamed.

Avoid Fixing: When youth experience messy feelings, our natural response is often to try to make the pain go away as quickly as possible. We rush to downplay the experience ("It's really not so bad.") or offer false reassurance ("Everything will be okay."). Often we attempt the quick fix by offering solutions, or worse, taking on the problem as our own and solving it for them. These responses often make things worse. They give youth the message that they are overreacting, their experience is trivial, and they are incapable of solving their own problems.

Develop an Authentic Youth-Adult Coaching Partnership

A true partnership exists when each person has the opportunity to make suggestions and decisions, and when everyone's contribution is recognized and valued. A youth adult partnership exists when adults see young people as full partners on issues that affect them.

We live in a society that does not give young people many opportunities to make their own decisions. The idea that children should be seen and not heard is still common for many adults. You will discover (if you haven't already) that when given a proper forum, today's young people are full of ideas and energy to make positive change in their lives, communities, schools, and families. As the accepted "leaders" in society, it is often up to adults to create these opportunities for young people to show their talents and concern for their society.

To be effective partners, adults must respect and have confidence in youth. If they are truly sharing the power to make decisions with young people, it means adults are letting go of their traditional roles, listening rather than telling, and working with, rather than for youth. Giving young people the authority to make decisions and a platform to share their opinions is a way to show respect.

Meaningful Involvement - Assign meaningful roles to youth, not just token opportunities. Young people are suppose to learn from the experience, as they contribute a unique and valuable perspective to the process. You must be committed to integrating their suggestions and following up on their ideas.

Support and Empowerment - All people need to feel that they are contributing. Adults can help young people by creating meaningful and challenging opportunities. You must provide young people the skills they need to meaningfully participate. Remember this may be their first experience in a true coaching setting. Help them understand what is going to happen and how they can participate. Debrief experiences after they happen.

Flexible Schedules - Youth have different schedules and priorities than adults. Their school schedules need to take priority. They may also be involved in many other activities that are equally important such as sports, clubs, jobs, etc. Sessions with youth should be regularly scheduled but need to be flexible to allow time for school, work, family, and friends. Follow up with the young person if they do not attend a session. Youth appreciate knowing they were missed and may need encouragement to continue participation.

Reflection, Evaluation and Celebration - Be clear of the expectations of the young person and address challenges when they arise. Check in regularly and make adjustments as needed. Make sure the young person has tangible objectives to work on. It is also important for them to see the impact of their involvement. Most importantly celebrate successes as they achieve goals and milestone (small and large).

Designing an Alliance

Once the initial coaching space is set, designed alliance is continuous and ongoing. The youth and coach design the coaching space so that it is customized to specifically meet the needs of the youth. It is also a dynamic space, capable of changing over time so that it will continue to meet the youth's needs. Much of the coaching alliance happens in the initial meeting between coach and client.

The purpose of designing an alliance is to:

- Create a safe and courageous space for clients to share openly.
- Establish client trust of coach.
- Help the coach know how to work with the client in a manner that empowers the client.

While each coach will develop their own unique style over time, here are some guidelines to get you started. This conversation can take anywhere from 10 minutes to an hour.

Set the stage for the client: Coaching provides a unique opportunity to create a relationship by design, remember this concept is new to many of youth. Help them out by telling them what to expect.

Example:

> "One of the unique aspects of a coaching relationship is that it is a relationship of design. You are creating me as your coach, your ally, your champion. What we are going to do next is spend some time having you design how I can best work with you. You may already have some ideas of how you want me to work with you around certain areas. There may also be some places you are not yet sure how you want us to work together. We will use this time to lay some groundwork. As we work together we will continue to create how we want to work with each other. How does that sound?"

Begin the Design: The coach takes notes and prompts the youth with questions as needed. Some youth already have ideas about what they would like. Start there.

Here are some questions to ask the client:

- "What are you looking for in a coach?"
- "If this coaching were to have a huge impact in your life what would it look like?"
- "What else?"

Initial Discovery: As the client answers generally, begin taking the questions into specifics.

- "How do you stop procrastinating in your life?"
- "What is the best way for me to confront you?"
- "What are some of the things you do that go against what you really want?"
- "How do you want me to respond when you have not completed something you agreed to complete?"

Coach Expectation/Style: During this portion of the discovery session, it is appropriate for the coach to speak about what is important in the relationship for them. It is the coach's opportunity to ask for what he or she wants from the youth.

Example:

> "My style is pretty direct. I like to call things as I see them. For example, if I see that you are compromising a value that you identified as important in one of our initial coaching sessions I might say... Wait a minute. I'm not buying it. I know that authenticity is one of your top values and what you just said doesn't fit that. What's really going on here? "Do I have your permission to be direct?"

Remind the client that the process continues throughout the coaching relationship and encourage the client to redesign over the course of the coaching partnership.

Example:

> "We have a great start here in how we will work together. I want you to know that this does not stop here. I invite you to keep designing as we go along. From time to time in the future, you will hear me check in and ask permission to tweak and change things. Will you continue to look at how we work together and give me feedback?"

Solidify the Coaching Relationship with a Formal Agreement

Now that you have set the groundwork it is time to put a formal agreement in place with the young person. The agreement is designed to confirm the expectations and formally acknowledge that the coach and youth are in agreement to begin the coaching relationship. Unlike other coaching agreements, the Authentic Youth Coaching agreement has a section where the youth can write in their specific commitment as discussed in the alliance session.

Sample Authentic Youth Coaching Agreement

This coaching agreement, signed this ____ day of _____, 20___; This agreement between_____ (Coach) and_____ (Youth/Client) whereby Coach agrees to provide Coaching Services for Client focusing on life skills and goals identified in the coaching sessions assessments and by the client.
Coaching Sessions

The services to be provided by the Coach to the Client are:

- Weekly face-to-face meetings.
- Telephone or Skype session(s) to be scheduled as mutually agreed upon between the Coach and the Client (or their parent/legal representative, if the Client is a

minor).
- Additional sessions can also be scheduled as mutually agreed upon.

Coaching Relationship

Coaching will be an ongoing relationship that may take a number of months, although either party can terminate the relationship at any time.

Throughout our working relationship, I will involve the youth in helpful conversations and/or other creative activities. Together, I and the Youth will work to help the Youth discover and achieve his/her goals.

With the Client's knowledge and support, and without violating confidentiality of specifics shared in the sessions, I will provide a verbal report to the Client's parent/legal representative (as applicable). This is done to assist the parent/legal representative in understanding the Client's progress as well as learning how they can continue to provide support and assistance to the youth.

Coaching Sessions

Coaching sessions are not therapy sessions or psychological counseling sessions, nor will any coaching sessions be a substitute for counseling, psychotherapy, mental health care or substance abuse treatment.

The Youth (or their parent/legal representative) will seek independent professional guidance for legal, medical, or mental health matters. If, in the course of coaching, I believe it would be more beneficial for the Client to pursue counseling or therapy, I will make that recommendation. The Client, or parent/legal representative, understands that all decisions in these areas are exclusively theirs, and I, as the Coach, acknowledge that decisions and actions regarding them are their sole responsibility.

Confidentiality

Coaching is a confidential relationship and I, as the Coach, agree to keep all information strictly confidential, except in those rare situations where the Youth's records might be subpoenaed by a court of law or where such confidentiality would violate the law. This can include, but is not limited to, thoughts of harming self or someone else, child abuse, elder abuse, etc. Otherwise, no information or materials will be shared with outside sources or other people regarding our coaching work, except with express written permission of the Youth (or parent/legal representative).

Other Details

1. This relationship is for a specific period of the Youth's choosing.
2. Each session will be in person, by phone or Skype and may last up to a maximum of 60 minutes. Emails are available between sessions.
3. 24-hour notice is requested for cancellation of a coaching session. "No-shows" unfortunately will not be refunded.

Youth Commitments:

1. _____

2. _____

3. _____

DISCLAIMER: The Youth (and parent/legal representative) is the sole decision-maker in the coaching process. Any and all actions or consequences resulting from the coaching sessions are the responsibility of the Client. The Client (and parent/legal representative) releases the Coach of all liability pertaining to the services rendered in the coaching relationship.

Signatures indicate agreement with this coaching agreement.

_____ Date___/___/_____
Client

_____ Date___/___/_____
Parent/Legal Representative (if applicable)

_____ Date___/___/_____
Life Coach

Step 2 - The Vision

In traditional coaching coaches are taught to start with an assessment but the Authentic Life Coaching starts with the visioning process and creating a vision board. Having the youth complete a visioning session allows them to visualize their future, write it down, and create a visual illustration of it. Visualizing generates a common goal, hope, and encouragement. It offers a possibility for fundamental change; gives the youth a sense of control; and generates creative thinking and passion. The vision board gets the youth excited and it helps them see where they want their life to go.

The visioning session can be done in an individual or a group setting. During the visioning session you are asking the youth to get the picture in their mind as you ask the questions. Explain that the object is to collect as many ideas as possible—nothing is too small, too big, or too crazy for consideration.

Tools you will need:

- The Visioning Journaling Sheet
- The Visioning Questions Worksheet
- Affirmation Worksheet
- Soft 'Spa-Like' & Upbeat 'Jazz-like' music

The supplies you will need for the vision board:

- Poster Board
- Glue/Glue Sticks
- Stack of Magazines
- Colored Markers/Glitter/Stickers (optional)

Visioning Session

Facilitating a visioning session in a group coaching session with other youth is good way to build rapport and youth seem to get more involved in the process. Here is an outline to implement a visioning session in an individual or group setting:

Intro:

"We're going to do an exercise that will help you define your personal vision: What you want to create for yourself and the world around you. I am going to guide you through a few steps to help you answer the powerful question: What do I really want? During this exercise, hold this space for yourself. Your vision can be deeply personal. You are not required to share it with anyone if you choose not to. But give yourself this gift. No cell phones/computers and no side conversations. Just be right here."

Preparing—Breathing: *[Play the spa-like music softly]*

"I'm going to ask you to start by giving yourself a little space."

> [Provide them with the "Visioning Journal Sheet" to write after the exercise, if in a group, ask them to spread out if they need to do so.]

I'm going to ask you to start by bringing yourself to a reflective frame of mind.... Take a few deep breaths.... Let go of any tension as you exhale, so that you are relaxed, comfortable, and centered.... As you take a few more deep breaths, center within....

Close your eyes, and think for a moment of a favorite place, a place where you are free, and happy. Stay with that image for a moment.... (1 minute)

Creating Results:

"Imagine achieving a result in your life that you deeply desire."

For example, imagine that you are living where you most wish to live, what does your home look like, or that you have the relationships that you most wish to have, what does your mate look like?

Ignore how "possible" or "impossible" this vision seems. Imagine yourself accepting, into your life, the full manifestation of this result you most want.

Describe in writing or pictures the experience you have imagined, using the present tense, as if it is happening right now. What does it look like? What does it feel like? What words would you use to describe it?

   [5 minutes for writing on writing in their journaling worksheet.]

Reflecting on Results:

"Now, pause to reflect on what you just wrote or drew. Did you articulate a vision that is close to what you actually want?"

   [Allow Youth to Answer.]

"We often self-limit, not really believing we can have what we want, or not believing our desires matter, or not believing that our life allows us to create what we want. You may have known immediately what you want, or you may have drawn a blank."

Describing Personal Vision:

   [Have the youth answer the questions on the 'Vision Session' worksheet. Have them use the present tense, as if it is happening right now.]

"Feel free to adjust any categories that don't fit your needs. Continue until a complete picture of what you want is filled in."

Imagine achieving the results in your life that you deeply desire. What would they look like? What would they feel like? What words would you use to describe them?

If you could be exactly the kind of person you wanted, what would your qualities be?

What material things would you like to own?

What is your ideal living environment?

What is your desire for health, fitness, anything to do with your body?

What types of relationships would you like to have with family, friends, and others?

What is your ideal profession or career? What impact would you like your efforts to have?

What would you like to create in the arena of individual learning, travel, reading, or other activities?

What is your vision for the community or society you live in?

Imagine your life has a unique purpose, fulfilled only by you through what you do, your relationships, how you live. Describe that purpose as another reflection of your aspirations.

[15 minutes.]

Sharing In a One-On-One Coaching Session

Ask the youth: "If you could have your vision now, would you take it?"

Use this question to help the young person clarify what it is they really want.

"Assume you have it now. What does that bring you?"

Use this question to understand what's beneath the desire. Keep asking: what does that bring you, what does that bring you.

Pairing For Sharing In Group Coaching Session:

"Now, I'm going to ask you to work in pairs, to help each other expand and clarify your vision."

[Form pairs.]

Take turns interviewing one another. Ask your partner:

"If you could have your vision now, would you take it?"

Use this question to help clarify what it is you really want. Now ask your partner:

"Assume you have it now. What does that bring you?"

Use this question to understand what's beneath the desire. Keep asking: what does that bring you, what does that bring you.

[10 minutes each.]

Creating a Vision Board

Flip- [Play the upbeat jazz-like music] Have the youth flip through the magazines and select the images,phrases, or words from them. Instruct the youth to rip out anything that speaks to them, represent something that they desire to have or was identified during the visioning session. Instruct them not to ask why or try to figure out what they will do with the images just yet. Just instruct them to get the images that speak to them as they flip. No gluing yet! Let them have fun looking through magazines and pulling out pictures or words or headlines that speak to them. Let them have fun with it. Have them make a big pile of images, phrases and words.

Sort – Next have them sort through the images and begin to lay their favorites aside in a new pile. Sorting is all about their intuition. Ask them to take notice if any of the images don't feel quite right. If they don't really speak to them ask them to sit them aside.

Arrange – Have the youth lay the pictures on their poster board to give them a sense of how the board should be laid out. For instance, they might create a theme to each corner of the board: Health, Business, Spirituality, Relationships. Or they might want to lay the images randomly all over the board in no particular order or they might want to fold the board into a book that tells a story. The options are endless.

Paste - After they've arranged all the items in a way that works for them have them paste everything onto the board. Encourage them to take their time doing this.

Decorate – When they're done pasting all the images on the board, encourage them to add some decorative touches. They can paint on it, write words with gel pens and add glitter, too!

Add the YOUTH! (optional, but powerful) – Have the youth paste a photo of themselves in the center of the board. If they plan to add a picture of themselves to their board, have them leave space in the center of the Vision Board as they are arranging it.

Display – Have the youth post their vision board. It is recommended to display their Vision Board in a prominent place where they will see it regularly. They don't have to do this, because some youth are a little shy about their dreams. The vision board may be something that might help them get over their fear and help keep them focused on their goals and dreams.

Act – Encourage the youth to take conscious action in their daily life towards their goals and dreams. Let the youth know that the board will help shape the coaching relationship.

Affirm –Help them speak their vision in the form of an affirmation. Affirmations are short powerful statements that are designed to help youth focus on what they want in the future by speaking them in the present tense. This will help youth get 'present' with their vision. Assist youth by having them write affirmations on the Affirmation Worksheet. For example, "I am so happy and grateful now that I am a successful entrepreneur!" Encourage the youth to speak their affirmations daily.

Coaching Considerations:

What if an item on a youth's vision board seems unrealistic to the life coach?

A life coach should *never* tell a young person that his or her future vision is unrealistic! Rather, consider learning what about the vision appeals to the young person and use this information to discover other related and appealing visions. One may discover that a seemingly unrealistic goal is possibly attainable with clear and specific action steps.

What if a future vision contains undesirable or dangerous elements?

Avoid being judgmental and let the young person express his/her feelings about their future vision. Learn what about the vision appeals to the young person. By allowing the young person to express his or her views, the life coach is not necessarily agreeing that the vision is desirable or safe, but rather learns about the "reinforcers", that is, what he or she expects to get out of the vision. Knowing the "reinforcers" of a young person's future vision can help a life coach to understand why a young person engages in negative behavior and/or in negative thinking.

Step 3 - Keeping it Real

Now that the vision board is complete it is now time to start incorporating some 'formal' assessments and helping youth do a reality check. In this step you will introduce the Life Balance Wheel and the Strengths & Needs Assessment. This step helps youth identify where they are and how satisfied they are with the different aspects of their lives. The Life Balance Wheel is a simple and interactive way to get a snapshot of how the youth sees the various areas of their life. The Strengths and Needs Assessment helps identify the strengths and needs in the different life areas.

Tools you will need for this step:

- Life Balance Wheel
- The Strengths and Needs Guidance questions
- The Strengths and Need Reporting Form

Life Balance Wheel

The Life Balance Wheel is a powerful coaching tool; it is one of the most flexible coaching tools in your coaching toolbox. The "Life Balance Wheel" can be used in many different ways. It's an excellent tool for feedback for life coaching , set meaningful goals, assessing how far a client has come, analyzing current and future expectations, skills and knowledge gap identification and many more and it can also be fun.

Have the youth think about each section of the wheel as it relates to their life right now. Have the youth assess each life area on a scale of 1 to 10 depending on how satisfied they feel about each area of their life in each area on the life wheel.

A score of 0 can be considered as unsatisfied (there is room for improvement) whereas a 10 is most satisfied (they are happy in this area). Encourage youth to be completely honest, so that you can identify the area's most needing attention and set goals to improve the key areas of their life.

Briefly explain the wheel and what it signifies to the youth. The Life Balance Wheel is a tool coaches use to get a snapshot of how satisfied a client is in their life. There are eight areas on the wheel. You may want to change the categories to reflect the areas of youth's life.

For example:

> The youth may choose to break the category of friends and family into two separate categories. The youth may wish to add a category, like adding school to career section.

Ask the client to rate their level of satisfaction in each of the areas.

> "I am going to ask you to rate your level of satisfaction in eight areas of your life. Zero means not satisfied and 10 means very satisfied."

- Have them place a dot on the number line in each area that represents their selection between 1-10.
- After the youth has rated each of the areas, ask them to connect the dots to form an inner wheel.
- This gives the client an overview of balance in their life.

Coaching Note: Remind the youth that it is not about getting perfect 10's. It's about a smoother ride. Remind them that, if this wheel were a tire on your car, how bumpy would their ride be?

- Listen to the youth's response
- Ask the youth, What area they would like coaching on or what area are they ready to make a change in?

- Once an area is selected, move towards the questions in the Strengths and Needs Assessment area that focus on the area they identified.

Strengths & Needs Assessment

Now that the youth has charted their life areas on the Life Balance Wheel and they've identified the areas would they like to start their coaching with use the Strengths and Needs Assessment (SNA) guiding questions to gauge the youth's strengths, needs, and interest in those areas. Use the Strengths and Needs Assessment Form to record the youth's responses. Make sure the SNA and the form are explained to the youth at the start of the session. The life coach does not sit down with a form to fill out but rather sits down with the youth for a friendly and open conversation in which strengths will be identified as the youth shares throughout the conversation. The life coach starts the conversation and guides it in the direction it needs to go to assess areas of strength as the youth continues to   communicate. *The Strengths & Needs Form is never to be given to the youth to fill out alone.*

Follow-up with powerful questions to focus in on possible areas of strengths and resources, as well as clarify ambiguous answers though the Motivational Interviewing techniques. In addition to helping youth focus in and pinpoint areas of strength, follow-up questions can also help keep the conversation flowing.

Because Strengths and Needs assessment continues to promote rapport building and emphasizes the young person's strengths, it is a great way to begin working with the young person and getting to know his/her environment. The challenge for the life coach is to remain open to the perspectives of the young person, his/her family, and other key people through the strengths and needs assessment rather than pursue the deficit trail that is often documented in the young person's records.

The life coach usually conducts strengths and needs assessments one-on-one with the young person. The process typically takes place over a series of sessions since it is important to have a "conversation" rather than an "interrogation." The conversation is not a straightforward conversation about areas of strength but more like a conversation that naturally flows, stopping at some areas of interest to discover more and naturally progressing onto other areas. The life coach should build the conversation from the content information and other background information provided by the youth, being sure to clarify and affirm as he/she contributes to the conversation.

The SNA sessions with the young person help the life coach to further develop the coaching relationship with the young person by building trust and starting to identify the young person's strengths and possible resources that may be available for them.

Whenever possible, the life coach assesses the additional possible areas of strength and resources surrounding the young person on an individual basis. This strength-based focus can help develop a foundation of the young person from which the young person is seen in a positive light.

Again, the Strengths and Needs Assessment is not a one-time assessment but rather an on-going process that continues as opportunities for open and honest conversations arise throughout the coaching relationship with the youth. Young people tend to reveal things over time, especially as trust is established. Therefore, there will be times when the young person shares information outside of the 'SNA session'.

Every coaching conversation can be educational and all information that could help support the young person and should be deemed important and should be recorded so that it is not lost.

The Strengths and Needs Assessment covers ten different areas that include:

1. Future Vision
2. Special Interest
3. Education
4. Employment/Career
5. Health
6. Personal/Social/Spiritual Development
7. Family & Friends
8. Living on Your Own
9. Transportation
10. Money Management

The primary purpose of Strengths and Needs Assessment is to identify strengths, interests, preferences and resources of the young person, his/her family, and other supportive relationships so an action plan can be developed with a strength-based focus that emerges through this assessment process. What one learns through Strengths and Needs Assessment includes the following information:

- What are the strengths, interests, and preferences of the young person in regard to his/her future?
- What resources are available or needed to assist the young person's successful transition?
- What goals and activities might the young person want in his/her transition action plan?
- Who can participate and how can they participate in goal setting and implementation.

Some of the information for the Strengths and Needs Assessment can be gathered in previous coaching sessions and from the youth's vision board session. Also continue to incorporate powerful coaching questions and motivational interviewing techniques to get a clearer understanding during these sessions. Guideline questions direct the coaching session, ensuring that the coach obtains information about the youth's interests, experiences, strengths, needs, and areas of interest in all areas. In addition to collecting important information, the Strengths and Needs Assessment helps to continue to build rapport with the youth. During the initial SNA session(s) the youth is engaged in a positive dialogue about his/her strengths, accomplishments, and current needs. Because the youth is an active participant in this part of the process, he/she is empowered to participate fully in the action plan that will come in later steps.

One challenge with the Strengths and Needs Assessment process is recording information as the conversation develops. The life coach will want to record the information that is shared but will need to keep the conversation flowing, as he/she is an active part of participating and listening. The life coach will need to operate a bit differently to successfully facilitate this type of 'conversation-based' assessment. Think of how a counselor conducts a session with a client. The counselor must take notes as the conversation unfolds but he/she must also guide the conversation as he/she listens and discusses relevant issues. The note taking during this assessment should be conducted much the same way. The life coach should take brief notes, only writing for very short periods of time, taking down just enough information to enable him/her to complete the Strengths and Needs Assessment profile later.

A good memory is especially necessary where conversations take place and extensive note taking is not possible. That is why being fully present in your session the youth is extremely important. As the life coach writes, he/she must continue to listen and interact, either keeping eye contact or using body language, e.g., nodding his/her head, to show he/she is still involved and listening. Using statements like "okay", "I understand what you are saying", and "tell me some more about that", as the life coach quickly jots down a few words, may be helpful to keep the momentum of the conversation going instead of allowing the conversation to cease while he/she writes.

Ways To Conduct An Effective Strength And Needs Assessment

- Conduct Strengths and Needs Assessment semi-structured conversations first with the young person before interviewing, one may gain the young person's trust and more easily by focus on the young person's perspectives.
- Utilize "reframing", a way of looking at each deficit from a strength-based perspective and describing the deficit as a skill or asset. Reframing helps the life coach and young person to stay focused on strengths and the future rather than on problems and the past.
- Adapt approaches for cultural influences. To engage young people and keep them engaged, a life coach will need to recognize the young person's and his/her family's culture and how the culture influences their decisions and actions.
- When applying the Strengths and Needs Assessment process, a life coach may need to modify the language used and the processes so that they are applicable to persons in diverse cultures and with varied linguistic heritage.

Strengths & Needs Assessment Questions

FUTURE VISION	
STRENGTH	NEED
What are your dreams / goals? What do you feel like is missing in your life right now that is important to you? What are you passionate about that give meaning to your life? What do you value that gives real happiness? Where do you want to be and what do you want to be doing in 5 years? 10 years? 20 years? What gifts that God has given to you that you are using effectively? What is it that you believe so strongly in that I would be willing to die for? Where do you seek inspiration, mentors, and working models for yourself? What do you want to be remembered for? What legacy do you want to leave?	What's not happening that I want to happen? Which gifts are you not using effectively?

SPECIAL INTEREST	
STRENGTH	NEED
How do you spend your free time? What are some things you like to do? What are your hobbies? What sports do you play? What musical Instruments do you play? Sing? Write poetry? What types of things do you read? (books, magazines, graphic novels) How do you spend your free time doings things with people who are important people in your life? What cultural activities do you participate in? What clubs or organizations do you belong to?	Are there any school subjects that you would like help with? Which ones? Do you get along with your teachers and classmates? What are some ways we can help you improve your school relationships? Do you need help setting or achieving your current educational goals? What help would you like? Do you need to develop educational plans after high school? What kinds of help would you like? Are you interested in finding our more about colleges, vocational programs in the area? Do you have any concerns about going to college or taking specialized training?

EDUCATION	
STRENGTH	NEED
What school are you attending now? What is the highest grade that you have completed? What do you like most about school? What are your favorite subjects? Who is your favorite teacher and what subject does he/she teach? What are your educational goals right now? What are your educational plans after high school/ GED? Have you contacted colleges or vocational schools in the area?	Are there any school subjects that you need help with? Which ones? Would you like to learn a second language? Do you need help setting or achieving your current educational goals? Do you need to develop educational plans for after high school? Are you interested in finding out more about colleges, vocational programs in the area? Do you have any concerns about going on to college or taking specialized training?

HEALTH	
STRENGTHS	NEEDS
How would you rate your physical health?	Are you concerned about any health problems?
Where do you go for health care and check-ups?	If you are taking medications, do you need to find out more about them?
When did you last see a doctor and a dentist?	Would you like to start a fitness program?
What type of regular physical exercise do you get?	Would you like to gain or lose weight?
Are you happy with your weight/current fitness?	Would you like learn more about:
Have you ever:	• Scheduling medical appointments?
• Called to make your own medical appointments?	• Using a thermometer?
• Used a thermometer to take your temperature?	• First aid?
• Taken a first aid course?	• CPR?
• Taken a CPR course?	• Birth control?
• Learned about birth control and sexually transmitted diseases?	• Preventing STD's?
• Used birth control?	Do you need to find out more about your medical history and your family's medical history?
Do you have a copy of your own medical history and your family's medical history?	

PERSONAL/SOCIAL/SPIRITUAL DEVELOPMENT	
STRENGTHS	NEEDS
What do like most about yourself? If your best friend were here, how would he/she describe you? Are you comfortable with meeting new people? Are you comfortable speaking up for yourself at home, school, work, or with friends? Everyone gets angry from time-to-time. What kinds of things make you angry? What do you do when you get angry? Is there a special adult mentor or resource person in your life that can help you with personal issues? If so, what are their names? Do you belong to any organizations or groups that help you spiritually or emotionally? Which ones? Does religion play a part in your life?	Is there anything about yourself that you wish were different? What? Would you like to feel more comfortable: Meeting new people? Speaking up for yourself at home, school, work, or with friends? How can we help you feel more comfortable? Would you like to learn other ways to manage your anger? Would you like to have more people in your life to help you deal with personal issues? Would you like to join or participate in an organization that could help you spiritually or emotionally?

FAMILY & FRIENDS	
STRENGTHS	NEEDS
Who do you call family? What are their names and relationships to you? How is your family involved in helping you prepare for life on your own? In what ways are you helpful to your family? Who are your friends? What are their names? In what ways are you a good friend to others? Which friends and family members would you go to for help? Do you have someone you consider to be a mentor? If so, who? Do you have or have you ever had or hope to have a dating relationship? Are you satisfied with your ability to develop, maintain or end those special relationships? Do you have or have you thought about having children of your own? What are your plans for marriage and family?	Are you satisfied with your relationships with your family? What if anything would you like to change? What are some ways your family could help you now? Are you satisfied with your relationships with your friends? What, if anything, would you like to change? Would you like to develop new friendships? Would you like help in beginning, ending, or managing a dating relationship?

LIVING ON YOUR OWN	
STRENGTHS	NEEDS
When do you think you will move out on your own? Where do you think you will live (city, part of the state, type of housing, etc.)? Do you think you will have a roommate or live alone? Do you have a network of supportive people who will help you when you are on your own? What do you think you will like best about living on your own? What do you think you will like least? What are some things that you have accomplished so far that will make it easier to live on your own?	Would you like to find out more about the housing options available to you? Would like help in developing a network? Would you like to learn how other young people have successfully moved out on their own? What do you need to accomplish before you move out?

TRANSPORTATION	
STRENGTHS	NEEDS
How do you get around now? Can you usually arrange your own transportation for job interviews, work, school and doctor's appointments? How do you plan to get around when you are on your own? Have you ever: • Taken driver's education? • Used public transportation to get where you need to go? What forms of public transportation? Obtained a driver's license?	Will you need help in getting independent living skills support? What kind of help do you need? Will you need help in carrying out your plan for transportation when you are on your own? Are you interested in: Taking driver's training? Learning about other forms of transportation? Getting a driver's license?

MONEY MANAGEMENT	
STRENGTHS	NEEDS
Do you have an allowance or other spending money? Would you say you manage that money well? Do you purchase your own clothing and personal care items? Are you usually pleased with your purchases? Have you ever: • Purchased a money order? • Written a check? • Opened a bank account? • Saved up money for a big purchase? • Filed an income tax form? • Paid your own bills? What kind? • Made out a budget for your own living expenses?	Would you like to get better in managing your spending money? Do you need to start a savings plan? What would you be saving for? Would you like to learn more about: • Money orders? • Writing checks? • Bank account • Saving money for big purchases? • Filing taxes? • Paying bills • Making out a budget

Step 4 - Got Skills?

This step helps identify and assess the youth's life skills areas. The Casey Life Skills Assessment (CLSA) is a free, online youth-centered tool that assesses life skills youth need for their well-being, confidence and safety as they navigate towards adulthood.

The Casey Life Skills Assessment also measures youth confidence in their future and their permanent connections to caring adults. It is appropriate for all youth ages 14 to 21 regardless of living circumstances (i.e., in foster care, with bio-parents, in group homes or other places). The assessment has 113 assessment items categorized within eight areas for skills, knowledge and awareness. Youth can complete the assessment in its entirety in approximately 30-40 minutes. Administering the Casey Life Skills Assessment will help youth identify their life skills strengths and needs in an interactive way.

It aims to set youth on their way toward developing healthy, productive lives. The assessment covers the following areas:

- Daily Living (17) – Meal planning and preparation, cleaning and food storage, home maintenance and computer and internet basics.
- Self Care (17) – Healthy physical and emotional development such as personal hygiene, taking care of one's health and pregnancy prevention.
- Relationships and Communication (18) – Developing and sustaining healthy relationships, cultural competency and permanent connections with caring adults.
- Housing and Money Management (23) – Banking and credit, finding and keeping affordable housing, budgeting and living within one's means.
- Work and Study (20) – Basics of employment, legal issues, study skills and time management.

- Career and Education Planning (9) – Planning for career and postsecondary education pertinent to older youth.
- Looking Forward (8) – Youth's level of confidence and internal feelings important to their success.
- Permanency (20) – Embedded within all of the skill areas of the assessment are items that assess a youth's connection to trusted adults, community of support and overall interdependent connections.

Below are coaching guidelines for preparing, administering and reviewing the assessment results with a youth.

Motivate youth to take the assessment: Be enthusiastic and positive about the assessment and its purpose. Make sure that youth know that it is a tool for them to use to learn what knowledge and skills they have and need. Let them know that you and others will work with them to use the information from the assessment to develop a plan to meet their wants, needs, and goals.

Encourage active participation: Invite them to share what they hope to get out of completing the assessment. Let them know this is an excellent opportunity for them to practice making decisions about their future what they want to do tomorrow, next week, and next year.

Once they have completed the assessment, review the youth's assessment results with them: The "At-A-Glance" page will show their average scores. The average score for each life skill area, including permanency, will be shown on a scale ranging from 1 – 5, with 1and 2 indicates an area of need, 3 indicates there is room for development, and 5 indicates high strength. Coaches can quickly see where a youth's strengths are, as well as areas where there are gaps in knowledge and proficiency. The next section of the assessment results will list all of the statements for a particular skill area and the youth's responses. This will help you identify specifically what the youth knows and doesn't know. A coach should review these areas with the youth. Follow up as necessary to be sure that the youth does fully understand these areas.

Invite caregivers in a youth's life to complete an assessment (optional but highly recommended): Caregivers who know the youth (i.e., foster parents, social workers, teachers, etc.) can also assess the youth's strengths and challenges using the CLSA. Explain to youth and their caregivers how getting this additional perspective can add to a rich conversation, open doors for productive communication that might not happen otherwise and gain additional "buy in" and support for the youth's coaching and learning plan activities.

Engage youth in a conversation about the results of their assessment: Share a copy of the results with the youth for the conversation and let them tell you about what the results mean. Start with the positive. Ask the youth to start by identifying their strengths, those areas where their average scores are closer to 5. Then move to looking at lower average scores. Ask the youth where they felt unsure and where they think they need help, what is challenging for them right now? Ask if there were any surprises for them in the results, if so, discuss why.

The Life Skills Results Coaching Session Outline

Once the youth has completed the assessment and has a copy in front of them, guide them through interpreting their own results. If an adult supporter/caregiver also completed an assessment on behalf of the youth this is an great opportunity to include them in the session.

Strengths (Always start with the strengths)

- Ask "What do you see as areas of strength?"
- Take the position of "I didn't know you knew all that."
- You can ask, "How specifically do you do that?"
- Ask "What is the first step...second step?" Youth will often have difficulty with sequences and may need help with this.

Challenges

- Ask "What do you see as areas of challenges?"
- "What specifically do you need to improve on in this area?"
- "How might the skills or strengths you already have help you with the challenging areas?

Disagreements (between the youth and caregiver results)

- Ask "Where do you see the greatest disagreement in perceptions?"
- Ask "What might be some reasons for the differences that you see here?'
- Ask the youth "What do you think you could do to demonstrate your skill in this area?"
- Ask the caregiver "What opportunities can you provide the youth to demonstrate his/her skill in this area?"

Setting Goals

- *Ask* the youth "Where do you want to start? Which life skills domain do you want to focus on?
- *Ask* the youth "Which section of the domain do you think is most important for you to work on?
- Ask "What life skill area will you need help learning that would help you achieve your goals?"

Remember that the goal is to work with the youth to develop a learning plan that is relevant to the youth and will give them some quick successes.

During the life skills coaching session, remember the following:

- Ask, don't tell.
- Listen to the answers.
- Start where the young person is.
- Avoid starting questions with "why." Try using "what" and "how" instead.
- Keep the conversation present and future focused.

Coaching Notes:

- Remember the best expert on a youth's knowledge and behavior is the youth. There will be exceptions where young people are incapable of self-reflection or self-perception because of psychological, physical or developmental challenges, and the additional perspective of a caregiver assessment is especially helpful. In most cases, however, youth are very capable of offering self-reports on what they know and can do.
- If the youth has taken the assessment before, compare results to previous assessment results. Again, start with the positive and first look for the areas of most improvement. It is important to note that sometimes a youth's scores may be lower than their first assessment.

They may have been overly confident in a particular skill, given answers because they thought they were the expected answers or simply guessed. Discuss why the scores are the same or different. Ask the youth if they feel more or less confident in particular areas.

- Life skill areas can be taken individually to avoid assessment fatigue. You can have the youth complete one area at a time and coach them on one area before moving on to the next skill area.

Step 5 - Who's Got Your Back?

Helping Youth Establish "Post-System" Connections

This step is about helping youth identify their support and 'creating' their family. Youth who age out of foster care may not have the support of their birth families but may have met some people along the way that they now consider family. This is about locating a supportive 'lifetime' family. For young people transitioning out of foster care, planning for permanence should be youth-driven, family-focused, continuous, and approached with the highest degree of urgency.

Permanence is not a philosophical process, a plan, or a foster care placement, nor is it intended to be a family relationship that lasts only until the youth turns age 18. Rather, permanence is about locating a supporting lifetime family. Permanence should bring physical, emotional safety and security within the context of a family relationship and allow multiple relationships with a variety of caring adults. Ensuring young people in foster care have both permanent relationships and life skills for independence is critical to their future well-being.

Permanence is achieved with a family relationship that offers safe, stable, and committed adult support, unconditional love, lifelong support, and legal family membership status. Permanence can be the result of preservation of the family, reunification with birth family; or legal guardianship or adoption by kin, fictive kin, or other caring and committed adults.

Permanency:

- Is safe and meant to last a lifetime.
- Offers the legal rights and social status of full family membership.

- Provides for physical, emotional, cognitive and spiritual well-being.
- Assures lifelong connections to extended family, siblings, other significant adults, family history and traditions, race and ethnic heritage, culture, religion and language.

Elements of Youth Permanency

A permanent connection with at least one (or more) committed adult(s) who provide a safe, stable and secure a positive supportive relationship, love, unconditional commitment, lifelong support, a legal relationship if possible and also provides the opportunity to maintain contacts with important persons, including siblings.

Achieving permanency requires the optimal balance of physical, emotional/relational, legal and cultural dimensions of permanency within every youth's array of relationships.

Physical permanency relates to a safe and stable living environment. *Emotional/relational permanency* relates to the primary attachments, family and other significant relationships that offer trust and reciprocity. Legal permanency relates to the rights and benefits of a secure legal and social family status. Cultural permanency relates to a continuous connection to family, tradition, race, ethnicity, culture, language and religion.

What does permanency mean to youth?

Permanency for youth is not necessarily the living arrangement. It is not simply providing independent living services, and it is not just offering adoption. It is providing that youth with life-long permanent connections to people the youth identifies as important to him/her. When asked, "What does permanence mean to you?" youth responded:

- "It means having your side of the church full when you get married." (Youth Presenter, Iowa Permanency Forum 2005).
- "It means having the key to the house." (Youth Participant, National Child Welfare Resource Center for Youth Development (NCWRCYD) Youth Permanency Forum 1999).
- "It means having your picture on the wall in someone's house." (Youth Narrator, Minnesota Adoption Exchange Video 2005).

As a life coach your main focus will be on helping youth identify, develop and maintain a balance of physical, emotional, and relational permanence. Incorporating the following tools is a very important to developing a plan with the youth. As a coach you will now be able to help youth identify their supports in helping them achieve their goals.

The tools you will need for this step are:

- Circles of Support Wheel
- Permanency Pact
- Casey Life Skills - Permanency Results

Circles of Support

Have the youth write in the names of people that fit in each category:

1. Circle of intimacy (inner)

This is the innermost circle and includes the people closest to the youth. This may include family members and/ or some of their oldest and dearest friends, former foster parents or pseudo/'play' foster brothers and sisters they have met through their foster care journey. The people in the inner circle are the people youth can't imagine not being around even if they don't see them all that often.

2. Circle of friendship (second layer)

The second circle includes the people they think of as friends in the real sense of the word. People they confide in, rely on, borrow money from, laugh and cry with, people who 'almost' made the inner circle.

3. **Circle of participation (or association) (Third Layer)**

The third circle includes all the people they are in contact with on a daily basis, people they work with in their places of employment, school friends, people who they meet when following their hobbies or interests (sports teams and school clubs), people who always say "hello" even though they only know their first name.

4. **Circle of exchange (Outer Layer)**

This outer circle includes all the people who are PAID to be in the youth's lives, either directly by an agency or because they provide them with a service. This might include their case/social worker, therapist, doctor, dentist, hairdresser, and plumber. Most paid support workers will fit in this circle as well.

Coaching Note: Review the youth's Casey Life Skills Permanency results and ask if any of the adults that they indicated as a connection on those statements are in the circle of support, if not encourage the youth to place them in the circles.

Permanency Pacts

Again, permanency is a stable, lasting, unconditional, emotional and relational connection that one has with family members and significant people in their lives, whether or not the youth resides with them. When youth have   trusting connections with adults who care about them and their success, this gives them optimism and encouragement that help them grow and learn. When youth transition from the assistance provided by programs and services, permanent relationships continue and provide support.

The Foster Club's Permanency Pact is a free tool that helps facilitate conversation between youth and identified supportive adults that can help youth achieve tangible connections and supports. The Permanency Pact provides a list of 45 tangible suggested supports that can help with this process. Together with the youth, the coach can then begin to develop a list of adults who may be able to provide some of those supports. This list may include people they identified in their circle of support and current relationships with adults and with whom the youth has had a previous connection that they wish to re-establish.

The Coach:

- Assists the young person in connecting the people they identified in the circle of support and on the Casey Life Skills Assessment to tangible supports in the permanency pact,
- Makes initial contact with the identified adult(s),
- Updates them regarding the youth's current situation,
- Gauges their level of interest,
- assists the adult in identifying possible supports they will provide, and
- Schedules and facilitates the Permanency Pact session.

Working with supportive adults, the Life Coach uses the list o f 45 Suggested Supports to draft a list of supports that confirms or further identifies the support the adult wishes to offer the youth. The list is then presented to the youth who will acknowledge the offer and accept those supports they feel would be most beneficial to the them. Either the youth or the supportive adult may suggest additional supports during this process.

The final list may be handwritten using the Permanency Pact list or entered into the Permanency Pact Certificate template. The youth and supportive adult signs the Pact and the Life Coach provides a witness signature. Copies of the Permanency Pact certificate are provided to the youth, the supportive adult, and maintained as a part of the youth's coaching portfolio.

Coaching Notes:

- Taking a step towards a trusting relationship is often a very great accomplishment for a youth with a background where relationships are broken, promises are often not kept, and disappointment in adults prevails. During this session strongly emphasize to the adult the importance of this commitment to the youth.

- To symbolize the importance of the commitment, it is recommended that a Permanency Pact be held in conjunction with some sort of ceremony or celebration. The Supportive Adult may want to give the youth a token keepsake gift (a piece of jewelry, photo frame, watch, engraved item, a special note, photo album, etc.).

- A Permanency Pact can be completed with each supportive adult who has been identified in a youth's circle of support, if desired.

Step 6 - The Master Plan

Now that you have worked through the previous steps, you now have enough information to start the Individualized Interactive Transitional Action Process (i²TAP). The key components of this process is that it must be interactive and individualized. Interactive in that it must be lead by the youth and provides the youth an opportunity to demonstrate what they have learned when in comes to life skills development as well as an opportunity to implement a new habit (i.e. savings toward a goal), or personal responsibility/leadership (i.e. making their own doctor's appointment and getting to the appointment on time). Individualized in that it must be based on the the youth's desires and goals. This step also involves working with the youth and their support system to develop their plan for the future and identifying a youth's goals, supports, life skills, and actions required to achieve the identified goals.

The purpose of the Individualized Interactive Transition Action Process (i²TAP) is to help youth set and achieve goals in education, housing, permanency, employment outcomes and etc., leading toward self-sufficiency, goal achievement, and support from the identified support system. The i²TAP is an action plan process based on the goals a youth identifies for him/herself, in   partnership with the life coach and identified supportive adults. The i²TAP should be a jointly created by the youth and the youth identified transition support team working together.

The best and most effective action plan is the one that a youth will actually implement. To get youth "buy in" develop the plan with active input from the youth, areas identified on their vision board, strengths and needs assessment, the results of their life skills assessment and other coaching tools used in the previous steps. Let youth lead the way in determining which goals and life skills domains are most important to them and choosing what goals they want to work on first. The primary component of the i²TAP is to ensure youth "voice and choice ". Below are the three   things that need to be kept in mind when implementing the i²TAP

1. Driven or guided by the young person.
2. Developed collaboratively with the input from the youth's supportive adults.
3. Based on the young person's strengths and meets the young person's needs.

Tools you will need for this step:

- Foster Club's Transition Toolkit
- Vision Board
- Strengths & Needs Results/Notes
- Casey Life Skills Assessment Results
- Permanency Pact Identified Supports

Again, the best place to start is in the areas the youth identifies. If the youth is unsure about where to start revisit the Vision Board, Casey Life Skills, and information gathered through the Strengths and Needs Assessment to help them decide. If you are using the Casey Life Skills building on the youth's strengths start in the life skills areas when the youth scored the highest and pay attention to the statements in that section where they answered "no", "mostly no", and " somewhat".

The life coach will use the Foster Club's toolkit sheets to assist the youth in developing their plan. The Foster Club Toolkit is a free downloadable resource that puts youth in control of planning their future. The toolkit sheets are designed to assist the youth in helping them successfully transition into adulthood. It is also a good tool to use as you track a youth's progress towards their goals in coaching sessions.

Every life area in the toolkit contains youth-friendly instructions. The life coach and youth utilize the sheets as they work toward their goals. The Foster Club Transition Toolkit is built around ten life areas and is aligned with the Casey Life Skills Assessment life skills areas. Each one can be easily incorporated in the coaching sessions. Each toolkit sheet also has a checklist. The checklist is a great way to help youth identify what they have and will need to be successful in each area. It also helps youth identify the important components, documents and forms of information needed to be successful in each life skill and goal area.

CLS Domains	# of CLS Items	CLS Assesses for	Transition Toolkit Sheets	Foster Club Transition Sheet Captures
Daily Living	17	Meal Planning and Preparation, cleaning and food storage, home maintenance and computer and internet skills	Life Skills	Information regarding safety, legal issues, etiquette, recreation/leisure, grocery shopping, cooking, cleaning, personal hygiene, and positive communication.
Self Care	17	Healthy physical and Emotional development such as personal hygiene, taking care if one's healthy and pregnancy prevention	Self Care Health	Information regarding health, mental health, dental, vision and prescription, insurance coverage and providers; and health education resources, such as substance abuse, coping with stress, nutrition, healthy relationships, pregnancy prevention and sexual health, fitness, first aid, and health self-advocacy.
Relationships & Comm.	18	Developing and sustaining healthy relationships, cultural competency and permanent connections with caring Adults	Health Community and Culture Social Life	Information regarding spiritual supports, peer supports, voter registration, selective Service registration, and ethnic affinity groups.
Housing & Money Mgmt.	23	Banking & Credit, finding and keeping affordable housing, and living within one's means	Finances & Money Housing Transportation	Information regarding banking; sources of government support, budgeting, credit checks, financial education on and Individual Development Account

Work & Study	20	Basics of Employ-ment, legal issues, study skills, and time mgmt.	Education Job & Career	Information on high school diploma higher education/ training plan; reading skills; math skills; writing skills knowledge of resources; current employment, listing of past employment résumé and/or sample application employment skills, knowledge of resources
Career & Education Plan	9	Planning for career and post-secondary education pertinent to older youth	Job & Career	Information on current employment; listing of past Employment; résumés and/or sample application; employment skills; knowledge of resources
Looking Forward	8	Youth's level of confidence and internal feelings important to their success		
Permanen-cy	20	Assesses a youth's connection to trusted adults, community of support and overall interdepend ent connections.	Permanence	Captures current legal permanency plan; identify supportive adults;Biological relatives

	Identity	Information on birth certificate; state-issued ID; Social security card
		citizen docs (if applicable); safe personal filing system

As you coach youth through the toolkit worksheets have them to map out their plan in the following areas:

What is my Goal: Help them clearly articulate the goal.

What I Have: Help the youth identify what they already possess or have completed towards achieving the goal.

Resources Available to Me: This is where the youth and coach can identify the available and needed resources to achieve the goal.

My Support Team: This is where the youth identifies the people who will help them towards the goal (i.e. case worker, foster parent, mentor, coach, permanency pact identified supports). The person should be named specifically in the plan.

This is My Plan: This is where the coach assists the youth with writing out the plan to achieve the goals in that area in measurable and actionable steps.

- Short Term Goals
- Steps & Services (and who will help me)
- Progress

Goals: Each goal and step should have a completion date the steps should lead up to the goal completion date.

Life Skills Goal: This is where you help identify the life skills that need to be developed in order to achieve the goal.

Readiness Scale – This is a scale that will help the youth determine how prepared they are in an area. As you coach youth in various areas you want to make sure as a part of a wrap up in the coaching session you want to check in with them and have them assess their readiness on a scale from 1-10. This will be helpful to track their progress.

You will utilize the toolkit planning sheets to assist a young person with describing and communicating how they will achieve their goals in each area. Ask powerful coaching questions to assist a young person in defining the life they want to lead.

For example, one might ask "If you could have your life going like you want in four months, what would it look like?" Use a time frame that will most motivate the individual (e.g., 4, 8, or 12 months.) Or, one might ask "How might you picture yourself as a college student in the fall?" After the goal is clear and understood, the life coach asks questions to assist the young person in "seeing" the action steps to achieve the goal. This process works best when the life coach uses what was learned in the previous steps to guide the process of attaining the goal.

Another example, "On your vision board you indicate you want to become a doctor. What could you be doing in the next four months that will help you pursue a medical career? What are some steps you could take?"

Utilize the Foster Club's Transition Toolkit Sheet planning in your sessions to assist youth and young adults in the following:

- Identify meaningful transition goals in one or many transition domains.
- Create a personalized plan of action that is likely to help him/her reach identified goals.
- Identify supportive community resources (people, programs, financial) that can be helpful to the young

person in attaining his or her transition goals.

- Access needed supports and resources.
- Identify appropriate timelines to meet the objectives.
- Develop self-determination and advocacy skills.
- Set goals and action steps, reviewing accomplishments, and celebrating successes.

Once the goals are identified it helps the youth move to discuss the actionable steps to achieve the goal. The outcome for each individualized goal is clearly written. All goals must be written in the same specific, measurable, action-oriented, realistic, and time-limited language (SMART). Large goals are to be broken down into smaller goals. Action steps should be achievable within a 2-3 week time frame. The completed transition toolkit sheets become the coaching roadmap, and portfolio.

Coaching Notes:

- It is important to remember that foster youth have had 'plans' throughout their foster care lives and the Foster Club Toolkit sheets are designed in 'Youth Friendly' terms and is 'their' plan for success.
- Remember this is not a 'case plan' and should never be referred to as one.
- Make sure the youth is provided with a copy and encourage them to bring their copy to the coaching sessions so as you are completing goals they can update their copy. This provides them a great sense of accomplishment and ownership.

Step 7 - Coaching to Achieve G.O.A.L.S.

The 7th step in the Authentic Life Coaching for Youth is about coaching youth towards reaching their goals. Remember the Authentic Life Coaching for Youth is a two-tiered approach. It is focused on helping youth gain the necessary life skills to successfully transition into life on their own as they pursue their goals. Foster youth who are transitioning into adulthood have a lot to juggle and with the right support, they will be able to achieve their goals and dreams. They will need action oriented coaching and a strong supportive network to help them. The Authentic Life Coaching for Youth tools and techniques are an integral part of helping change the lives of youth.

Tools you will need for this step:

- Completed Transition Toolkit Worksheets
- Strengths & Needs Assessment Notes
- Casey Life Skills Resources to Inspire Guide
- G.O.A.L.S. Coaching Worksheet(s)

G.O.A.L.S.

G.O.A.L.S. is a simple acronym that helps you coach youth towards their goals in every session:

- **G**oals
- **O**utcomes
- **A**ctions
- **L**ife Skills
- **S**upports

Now that you have coached youth through the gathering of information and the development of the plan now lets review a coaching session outline:

For this example the youth's **G**oal is to find and secure an apartment. You will review and discuss:

- Foster Club Transition Toolkit - Finances & Money and Housing Sections

Next discuss the desired **O**utcomes and **A**ctions needed to achieve the goal. This is where you discuss the desired outcome. The youth wants to move in 6 months so you begin to ask questions to help the youth get clear on the action steps and to set a target date. You will also discuss available resources that the youth has and if there are other supportive resources available.

Next identify the **Life Skills** that are needed in order to successfully achieve the goal. During the life skills assessment their Casey Life skills Assessment results indicated they answered the following in the Housing and Money Management section:

Somewhat to:
I know how to find safe and affordable housing.
I can figure out the costs to move to a new place, such as deposits, rents, utilities, and furniture.
I know how to fill out an apartment rental application.

No to:
I know how to get emergency help to pay for water, electricity, and gas bills.
I know what can happen if I break my rental lease.
I can explain why people need renter's or homeowner's insurance.

This is where you begin to work with the youth to outline the life skills development and what the youth will be able to do as a result of learning the skill as well as identify the training resources. Using the Casey Life Skills Resources to Inspire Guide will help you outline specific life skills competencies and life skills resources.

Life Skills Goal 1 Knows and understands the kinds of housing available in one's community.

Steps to get there:

- Identify two types of housing options (e.g., apartments, rooms for rent, houses, mobile homes, public or low income housing).

- Compare each housing option against one's personal needs and financial resources.

Life Skill Training Resources:

- I Can Do It! Finding My Own Place, p. 32.
- Ready, Set, Fly! Housing #8

Life Skills Goal 2 Can develop a plan to move into one's own living arrangement.

Steps to get there:

- Identify and calculate all start-up costs (e.g., application fee, security deposit, utility deposits, installation fees, first month's rent, furnishings and household items).

- Create a list of necessary items (e.g., furniture, kitchen equipment, towels and linens).

- Develop a realistic monthly budget for maintaining the living arrangement.

Life Skill Development Resources:

- I Can Do It, Starting out Supplies, p. 19-22.
- I Can Do It, Furnishing, p. 23-31.
- I'm Getting Ready, Equipment and Supply Checklist, PL-8,PL-9
- Money Management, Personal Budget, p. 9-63
- Start-up Costs, p. 64-69.

The Final Step is to identify the **Supports** needed to achieve the goal and the skills. As a coach your role is to help the youth identify the adult supports that will help them learn the skills and help them in securing an apartment in 6 months. Ask the youth to identify the supportive adult(s) who will assist them in achieving the life skills and goals. All of these steps can be outlined on the Foster Club Transition toolkit Life Skills, Money & Finances, and Housing worksheets.

Coaching Notes:

- Provide the youth with the life skills training resources and review them with the youth. As a part of their follow-up for the next session is to have them work with their identified supportive adult to teach them the skills.
- Remember your role as a coach is to help youth rely and enlist the support of the people they've identified to help them.
- The Transition Toolkit sheets become a part of the youth and coach's portfolio.

Keeping Focus During Your Coaching Sessions

Structuring purposeful interaction – All coaching sessions should begin with a specific session goal in mind. So at the end of the session both the youth and coach will know the purpose of the session was met. Prepare for your session with a topic but also be prepared if the youth needs to work through a real-time situation.

Using first-person pronoun – Making "I" statements – Encourage youth to speak in "I" statements – Keep them out of the 'blaming and encourage them to take personal responsibilities for their action and situations that they are involved in.

Keeping the focus and avoiding "topic jumping" – Encourage youth to stay on the initial topic of conversation.

Using past-present-future tenses in self-expression – When youth are expressing themselves make sure you are gauging whether they are speaking in past, present, or future terms. It is very important to keep youth in present and future terms.

Encouraging youth to see themselves with clarity – Youth sometimes speak in terms based on what others think and feels that the definitions of others define them. Ensure youth have a clear vision of who they are based on their defined qualities.

Giving directions – achieving clarity – As a coach give direction by asking clarifying questions. Remember 'Ask" and 'Don't tell' youth what to do.

Summarizing – Continue to summarize the focus during the conversation to ensure you are on the same page with the youth.

Forms & Worksheets

Visioning Journal Sheet

Visioning Session Questions

Affirmations Worksheet

Authentic Youth Coaching Agreement

Strengths & Needs Assessment Coaching Notes

Life Balance Wheel

G.O.A.L.S. Coaching SessionNotes

Visioning Journal Sheet

Date___/___/___

_____

_____

_____

_____

_____

_____

_____

_____

_____

_____

_____

_____

_____

_____

_____

_____

_____

_____

_____

Visioning Session Questions

Imagine achieving the results in your life that you deeply desire. What would they look like? What would they feel like? What words would you use to describe them?

If you could be exactly the kind of person you wanted, what would your qualities be?

What material things would you like to own?

What is your ideal living environment?

What is your desire for health, fitness, anything to do with your body?

What types of relationships would you like to have with family, friends, others?

What is your ideal profession or vocation? What impact would you like your efforts to have?

Affirmation Worksheet

I am so happy and grateful now _____

_____

_____

I am so happy and grateful now _____

_____

_____

I am so happy and grateful now_____

_____

_____

I am so happy and grateful now_____

_____

_____

I am so happy and grateful now_____

_____

_____

I am so happy and grateful now_____

_____

_____

Authentic Youth Coaching Agreement

This coaching agreement, signed this _____ day of _____, 20___, This agreement between: _____ (Coach) and_____ (Youth/Client)whereby Coach agrees to provide Coaching Services for Client focusing on life skills and goals identified in the coaching sessions and assessments.

Coaching Sessions

The services to be provided by the Coach to the Client are:

- Weekly face-to-face meetings. Telephone or Skype session(s) to be scheduled as mutually agreed upon between the Coach and the Client (or their parent/legal representative, if the Client is a minor). Additional sessions can also be scheduled as mutually agreed upon.

Coaching Relationship

- Coaching will be an ongoing relationship that may take a number of months, although either party can terminate the relationship at any time.

- Throughout our working relationship, I will involve the youth in helpful conversations and/or other creative activities. Together, I and the Youth will work to help the Youth discover and achieve his/her goals.

- With the Client's knowledge and support, and without violating confidentiality of specifics shared in the sessions, I will provide a verbal report to the Client's parent/legal representative (if the Client is a minor). This is done to assist the parent/legal representative in

    understanding the Client's progress as well as learning

how they can continue to provide support and assistance to their child.

Coaching Sessions

- Coaching sessions are not therapy sessions or psychological counseling sessions, nor will any coaching sessions be a substitute for counseling, psychotherapy, mental health care or substance abuse treatment.
- The Youth (or their parent/legal representative, if Client is a minor) will seek independent professional guidance for legal, medical, or mental health matters. If, in the course of coaching, I believe it would be more beneficial for the Client to pursue counseling or therapy, I will make that recommendation. The Client, or parent/legal representative, understands that all decisions in these areas are exclusively theirs, and I, as the Coach, acknowledge that decisions and actions regarding them are their sole responsibility.

Confidentiality

Coaching is a confidential relationship and I, as the Coach, agree to keep all information strictly confidential, except in those rare situations where the Youth's records might be subpoenaed by a court of law or where such confidentiality would violate the law. This can include, but is not limited to, thoughts of harming self or someone else, child abuse, elder abuse, etc. Otherwise, no information or materials will be shared with outside sources or other people regarding our coaching work, except with express written permission of the Youth (or parent/legal representative if Client is a minor).

Other Details

- This relationship is for a specific period of the Youth's choosing.

- Each session will be in person, by phone or Skype and may last up to a maximum of 60 minutes.
- Emails are available between sessions.
- 24-hour notice is requested for cancellation of a coaching session. "No-shows" unfortunately will not be refunded.

Youth Commitments:

1. _____
2. _____
3. _____

DISCLAIMER: The Youth (and parent/legal representative, if Client is a minor) is the sole decision-maker in the coaching process. Any and all actions or consequences resulting from the coaching sessions are the responsibility of the Client. The Client (and parent/legal representative) releases the Coach of all liability pertaining to the services rendered in the coaching relationship.

Signatures indicate agreement with this coaching agreement.

_____Date___/___/___
(Client)

_____Date___/___/___
(Parent/Legal Representative, if applicable)

_____Date___/___/___
(Coach)

Strengths & Needs Assessment Coaching Notes

FUTURE VISION	
STRENGTHS	NEEDS

SPECIAL INTEREST	
STRENGTHS	NEEDS

EDUCATION	
STRENGTHS	NEEDS

EMPLOYMENT/CAREER	
STRENGTHS	NEEDS

HEALTH	
STRENGTHS	NEEDS

PERSONAL/SOCIAL/SPIRITUAL DEVELOPMENT	
STRENGTHS	NEEDS

FAMILY & FRIENDS	
STRENGTHS	NEEDS

LIVING ON YOUR OWN	
STRENGTHS	NEEDS

TRANSPORTATION	
STRENGTHS	NEEDS

MONEY MANAGEMENT	
STRENGTHS	NEEDS

Life Balance Wheel

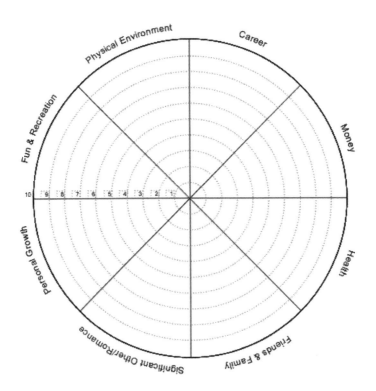

LIFE BALANCE WHEEL INSTRUCTIONS

The 8 sections in the Life Balance Wheel represent the areas of your life.

- Please change, split or rename any category so that it's meaningful and represents a balanced life for you.

- Next, taking the center of the wheel as 0 and the outer edge as 10, rank your **level of satisfaction** with each area out of 10 by drawing a straight or curved line to create a new outer edge (see example)

- The new perimeter of the circle represents **your** 'Wheel of Life'.

G.O.A.L.S. Coaching Session Notes

Youth Name:

Primary Skills Areas

Daily Living/ Home Management & Safety	Self-Care/ Health/ Nutrition	Relationships & Communications/ Personal Development	Housing & Money Management
Work/Study Life & Organizational Skills	Careers & Education	Permanent Connections	

Secondary Skills Areas

Food/Nutrition	Physical/ Dental Health	Developing Relationships
Home Cleanliness	Mental Health	Communication
Cooking	Medication Management	Cultural Competency
Laundry	Health	
Food Storage	Personal Benefits	Spirituality
Home Safety		Domestic Violence
Grocery Shopping	Personal Hygiene	Healthy Relationships
Meal Planning	Personal Safety	Etiquette
Meal Preparation	Sexuality Alcohol/Drug Prevention	Conflict/ Resolution
Bathroom Clean-up	Maintaining A Balance Diet	
Home Repairs	Sexual Education	
Utilizing Cleaning Products	Exercise	

Goals

Outcomes

Actions

Life Skills

Supports

Additional Notes:

Resources

- Strengths and Needs Questions
- Strengths & Needs Log
- Vision Board Sheet
- Visioning Session Journal Sheet
- Visioning Session Questions
- Life Balance Wheel
- Resources to Inspire Guide
- I Can Do It
- Ready Set Fly!
- PAYA – Modules I - V
- Foster Club Transition Tool Kit
  https://www.fosterclub.com/files/transition_toolkit.pdf]
- Foster Club Permanency Pact
  https://www.fosterclub.com/ files/PermPact_0.pdf]
- The Casey Life Skills Assessment [www.caseylifeskills.org]

Reference Materials

Ansell, Dorothy I. & Casey Family Programs Ansell-Casey life skills assessment (ACLSA) and life skills guidebook manual / edited by Kimberly A. Nolan, Michael Horn, A. Chris Downs & Peter J. Pecora. 2000

Authentic Youth Engagement: Youth-Adult Partnerships © http://www.jimcaseyyouth.org/authentic-youth-engagement-youth-adult-partnerships

Bell, John, Understanding Adultism: A Key to Developing Positive Youth-Adult Relationships - An outstanding Article That Helps Explore Adultism. Youth Build.

Bridges Transition Model- Guiding People Through Change www.mindtools.com/pages/article/bridges-transition-model.htm

Casey Family Programs. A Call to Action: An Integrated Approach to Youth Permanency and Preparation for Adulthood. April 2005. Casey Family Programs

Casey Family Programs Ansell-Casey life skills assessment: youth & caregiver level 4, version 4.0. 2005

Material adapted from: Ingersoll, Wagner & Gharib, 2000; NIAAA Project MATCH Motivational Enhancement Therapy manual (Miller, Zweben, DiClemente, & Rychtarik, 1992; Rosengren & Wagner, 2001

FosterClubTransition Toolkit©2010 FosterClub, Inc. and Foster-ingconnections.org.

Permanency Pact © 2006 FosterClub, Inc.

Powerful Coaching Questions Adapted from Co-Active Coaching

(3rd ed.) © 2011 by Henry Kimsey-House, Karen Kimsey-House and Phillip Sandahl

The Adolescent Brain: New Research and Its Implications for Young People Transitioning From Foster Care © 2011, Jim Casey Youth Opportunities Initiative

Scott, R. and Houts (1978). Strengths & Needs Assessment Adapted from Individualized Goal Planning with Families in Social Services. Currently part of New Jersey's Life Skill Assessment System, 1996, Dorothy Ansell and Joan Morse.

Positive Youth Development and Independent Living: Building Staff Competency and System Capacity Curriculum, Child Welfare League of America, 2001.

The National Resource Center for Permanency and Family Connections at the Hunter College School of Social Work http://www.hunter.cuny.edu/socwork/nrcfcpp/pass/learning-circles/

Transitions: The Rights. Respect. Responsibility.® Campaign Volume 14, No. 1, October 2001

Transitioning Youth From Foster Care to Successful Adulthood. Partners (Number 2, 2007) www.frbatlanta.org/

Made in the USA
Middletown, DE
19 September 2016